About the Northeast Conference

Established in 1954 as an outgrowth of the Yale-Barnard Conference on the Teaching of French, the Conference has focused on effective learning of languages, all those commonly taught in this country, ancient and modern, including English to Speakers of Other Languages.

In preparation for each annual Conference, the Chairman, with the approval of the Board of Directors, chooses a theme and appoints a team of authors to research and write on different facets of the theme. These essays comprise the Northeast Conference *Reports* which serve as the basis for the Conference, keynote speech, workshops, and panels. The *Reports* are mailed to preregistrants one month in advance of the Conference.

In addition to the concurrent and general sessions, there are preconference workshops, film and video showings, and exhibits of textbooks and other teaching aids. The Conference is supported by hundreds of schools, colleges, and educational associations. Representatives of these institutional members form the Advisory Council, whose members meet at the end of each Conference to elect new Directors.

Over the years the Conference has become the largest and most influential gathering of foreign language educators in the country. Some 3,000 teachers, chairmen, and supervisors from across the nation and many foreign countries now attend each annual meeting. The Northeast Conference has encouraged and aided the formation of other similar regional associations: the Southern Conference on Language Teaching in 1965 and the Central States Conference on the Teaching of Foreign Languages in 1968.

The Conference has numerous awards: among them are the annual Stephen A. Freemen Award for a published article on teaching techniques, the Foreign Language Advocate Award for contribution to the profession by an outsider, and the Northeast Conference Award for Distinguished Service and Leadership in the Profession presented in memory of Nelson H. Brooks.

The Northeast Conference is an organizational member of the American Council on the Teaching of Foreign Languages, the Joint National Committee for Languages, and the National Federation of Modern Language Teachers Associations.

NORTHEAST CONFERENCE ON THE TEACHING OF FOREIGN LANGUAGES

THE LANGUAGE TEACHER: COMMITMENT AND COLLABORATION

John M. Darcey, Editor
Christine L. Brown, Chairman
1987

Library of Congress Catalogue Card Number 55-34379
ISBN 0-915432-87-0

Contents

Introduction

The theme of the 1987 Northeast Conference is "The Language Teacher: Commitment and Collaboration." For this volume of the *Reports* we have focused solely on "collaboration." The *Reports* are not limited to collaborative efforts within the field of foreign language teaching; several explore ways in which we may collaborate with those outside our field.

Although many models of collaboration among language teachers have existed for many years and continue to exist today, we have been hesitant to form alliances with colleagues in other disciplines, administrators, parents, and business leaders. If we are truly to benefit from the latest efforts of educational reform and from an apparent renaissance of interest in foreign languages, we must now reach out to establish strong links with leaders outside our discipline and even outside of education.

The 1987 *Reports* are a departure from the past. Eight authors have accepted the challenge of writing about the broad context of education. They emphasize the increasingly strategic part which foreign languages may play as we prepare for the last decade of this century and the twenty-first century in which today's young people will spend the majority of their lives.

These distinguished individuals in the *Reports* have provided a view "through the looking glass" of language programs from kindergarten through adult education. They strongly suggest that we expand our realm of influence to include parents, school and college administrators, and business leaders. The authors have provided many suggestions for us. We hope that these insights and suggestions will serve as a blueprint for the 1990s and beyond.

The first Report, written by Claire Gaudiani, reviews important collaborative efforts within the field of foreign languages. The author gives specific examples of successful models such as the Academic Alliances and the Rockefeller Foundation fellowships. Tonkin then discusses foreign languages in colleges and universities and the importance of deans, provosts, college presidents, trustees, alumni, and parents in the success of language programs. He suggests possibilities for collaborative programs in international studies. In his Report he also describes the "compleat foreign language professor."

Ambach explains the New York State plan for global education which includes many elements of successful collaboration among the New York State Education Department, professional teacher organizations, members of the New York State Legislature, and the public. The New York State plan can serve as a model which other states may wish to examine, adapt, and even adopt.

The fourth and fifth Reports are written by superintendents of urban school districts. Both present model programs with strong foreign language components. One program, in Baltimore (MD), was developed because the district wanted to revise the curriculum to include a long sequence of foreign language study; the other one, in Pittsburgh (PA), is based on the magnet school concept and was originally proposed as a desegregation plan. Both models owe their existence and success to the strong initial and continuing support of teachers, parents, and school boards who worked together to formulate the plans and implement them.

Ehrlich and Hodych, two parents — one from California and one from Canada — stress the importance of the role of parents in foreign language programs. Ehrlich describes

Advocates for Language Learning (ALL), an organization of parents who support the early study of foreign languages; and Hodych reviews the successes of Canadian Parents for French which supports the study of French in bilingual and immersion programs in Canada.

In the final Report, Foster, who represents the corporate world, tells us how important properly trained foreign language majors can be in the business world. He points out that corporations are eager to hire people who have had the type of training which both Gaudiani and Tonkin espouse in their Reports.

We salute these authors who have generously shared with us their ideas for successful collaborative plans which have served to expand and strengthen the role of foreign languages in schools, colleges, universities, and businesses. We sincerely hope that this will be the beginning of long and fruitful collaboration with our friends in education and business.

Christine L. Brown, *1987 Conference Chairman*
Glastonbury (CT) Public Schools

John M. Darcey, *1987 Editor*
West Hartford (CT) Public Schools

CLAIRE L. GAUDIANI is a specialist in seventeenth century French literature and the history and philosophy of science of this period. She currently is writing her fourth book, a study of the impact of the Scientific Revolution on French literature of the seventeenth century. She has also authored a book on the cabaret poetry of Theophile de Viau and another called *Teaching Writing in the Foreign Language and Literature Curriculum*. She has recently completed a book on academic management and curricular design called *Strategies for Development of Foreign Language and Literature Programs*, published by the Modern Language Association and has also written articles on seventeenth century French poetry, foreign language pedagogy, humanities education, and management in higher education. Gaudiani has held research fellowships from the American Council of Learned Societies and the National Humanities Center.

She has taught at the University of Pennsylvania since 1981, where she is currently a Senior Fellow in Romance Languages and Assistant Director of the Joseph H. Lauder Institute for Management and International Studies. She received her undergraduate degree from Connecticut College and her M.A. and Ph.D. from Indiana University. She has served since 1979 on the National Board of the National Endowment for the Humanities and also consults for the Exxon Education Foundation and the Rockefeller Foundation.

She has designed and directed the NEH-Exxon Education Foundation "Workshops for Development of Foreign Language and Literature Programs" and the NEH-Rockefeller project called "Strengthening the Humanities Through Foreign Language and Literature Studies." She is currently director of "Academic Alliances: School/College Faculty Collaboratives," a project designed to build communities of scholars among teaching faculty in the major disciplines.

Claire L. Gaudiani

The Importance of Collaboration

Introduction

The environment for foreign language study has changed dramatically since the President's Commission in 1979. With the encouragement of the corporate community engaged in international management and riding on the tailwinds of discontent over dropping standards in American education, the foreign language and literature field has experienced a renaissance since the days of dropping language requirements. In this changed environment, foreign language teachers are no longer alone. Their efforts to move students from the early to advanced stages of language proficiency are boosted by new collaborations and new support from corporate officers, school administrators, university professors, and deans, as well as parents. Many members of these groups now recognize the urgent need for more Americans proficient in foreign languages. In addition, the work of language teachers is enhanced by the interest of specialists in theoretical linguistics, ESOL, artificial intelligence, and computer science, all of whose fields will increasingly bear fruit in the foreign language classroom in schools and colleges. Collaborations among leadership universities and colleges as well as among major foundations and political groups are increasingly affecting the availability of financial support for teachers of foreign languages. This is a whole new day for our field.

How appropriate that the Northeast Conference dedicate a volume to "Collaboration and Commitment." Both have gotten us where we are and both will continue to move the profession to a new level of prominence and productivity. Contributors to this volume offer a range of voices that language teachers need to hear to support their efforts.

Humphrey Tonkin, President of Potsdam College of SUNY, in his report "Grassroots and Treetops: Collaboration in Post-secondary Language Programs" makes a centrally important point: "Language study that leads only to the replacement of one ethnocentricism with a second has failed in its primary purpose: the expansion of our intellectual horizons to embrace the larger world."

Madeline M. Ehrlich and Carolyn Hodych remind us how important parents are in developing students' attachment to their study of foreign languages. Gordon Ambach's article reviews the changes in New York State's foreign language and international education policy—the results of a fortuitous combination of energy, wisdom, and foresight from the educational, political, and corporate sectors. Badi Foster expands the perspective from the corporate side by outlining the implications of the global economy for language faculty. Superintendent Pinderhughes gives a plan for the development of an ambitious venture: required foreign language studies for grades seven, eight, and nine in a large inner-city school district. Collaboration and commitment were needed from a wide range of teachers, administrators, and parents. Finally, another school superintendent, Richard Wallace, discusses the magnet school concept for foreign languages and international studies. These voices contribute to the growing sense of urgency about foreign language study. They also bear witness to the willingness of other adults to collaborate with foreign language teachers in their commitment to strengthening teaching in this field.

The Aspen Institute

Recently, the changing environment was further enhanced by the efforts of Richard Lambert, professor of sociology, University of Pennsylvania. With the support of four major foundations, Lambert convened 20 specialists in the foreign language and literature field at the Aspen Institute in June 1986, to work toward writing a national policy for the study of second languages in the United States. The profession faces a critical need for collaboration on common goals if we are to bring the United States to a new level of preparedness to meet its challenges and responsibilities in the global environment for the year 2000. The study group focused on the importance of better empirical research on language methodology to support teachers. It also stressed the need for more imaginative and productive teaching materials, particularly authentic materials made easily accessible to busy teachers. Finally, the group suggested that language teachers' work would be enhanced if more adults could expect to need and use languages in their professions. The adult-use focus of the agenda sets a new direction for the language and literature field. It emphasizes the critical importance of excellent teaching at earlier stages of language study and of articulation between levels of instruction from grade school to high school to college. The focus of attention in the foreign language teaching field has, until recently, been almost exclusively on the first two years of college foreign language study, with less attention on how to teach younger students most effectively or how to assure that adults would continue to use and sustain their second languages. Through active collaboration among school and college faculty, foreign language and ESOL faculty, among government, academic, and business sectors, and between parents and teachers in a range of different kinds of academic institutions, the study of foreign languages will occur in a new environment in the future — an environment conducive to advancement toward professional levels of proficiency in second languages for American students.[1]

While working toward a national policy for foreign language study field, Lambert has also focused on the development of a National Center for Second Language Pedagogy. This center, located at the School of Advanced International Studies at The Johns Hopkins University, creates a central site for the coordination of research and experimental programs designed to improve the teaching of languages. The national center has received funds from Exxon Education Foundation, the Pew Memorial Trust, and the Ford Foundation. Working together in teams, school and college faculty and researchers have the best chance to evaluate current methodology, develop improved approaches to language teaching and the assessment of skills, strengthen teacher education, cope with differences among language learners as well as among language families, and develop improved teaching materials. According to Lambert:

> Center-sponsored activities will have three guiding principles:
> - they should be "applied," that is they should be directly related to the improvement of the foreign language competency of Americans, particularly adult Americans, and to lifting a more substantial number of them to a genuinely high level of skill,
> - they should reflect an empirical orientation, constantly measuring practice against outcomes,
> - they should bridge the various segments of the language teaching community and link them to social scientists and those in public policy and administration whose participation is essential to the upgrading of our national pool of foreign language competencies.
>
> The initial tasks which the Center will undertake will be to:
> 1 develop a comprehensive national policy on foreign language teaching,
> 2 determine research priorities tied to national objectives which would guide public and private funding sources, as well as the Center's own research,
> 3 foster the development of innovative instructional methodologies aimed at increasing the effectiveness of teachers and language learners in both the public and private sectors,
> 4 initiate a limited number of key high leverage projects to inform the policy process and serve as prototypes for more general developments in the field.
>
> The Center will engage in research, materials development, training, diffusion, articulation and evaluation. It will serve the needs of teachers and learners at the various educational levels and users of language skills in business, government, education, research, public affairs. The inclusion of this range of audiences insures a rich and encompassing research agenda which, in turn, will lead to a patterned understanding and improvement of teaching and learning foreign language skills.
>
> Only part of this ambitious national effort will be carried out on the site of the Center itself. A great deal of the work will be carried out by participating centers on the campuses of other institutions, by national membership organizations, and by individuals who have the substantive expertise to contribute to the tasks. Indeed, the activities sponsored by the Center will regularly represent a flexible mixture of those carried out at headquarters and those conducted elsewhere, all of them dedicated to the same core national agenda (Richard D. Lambert, "Proposal to Create a National Foreign Language Center").

National Endowment for Foreign Language

Yet another collaborative venture lies before the language teaching profession. Under the auspices of the American Association of Universities, documents are being prepared to designate federal funds for a National Endowment for Foreign Languages and International Studies. This endowment on a par with the National Endowment for the Humanities (NEH) and structured like the National Science Foundation is intended to become a permanent unit within the United States government and stand as an indication of the dedication of the United States to achieve preparedness in meeting its second language obligations in an international environment. Currently, the collaboration of academic and government leaders is developing the necessary background papers to write the legislation designed to bring this new endowment to the attention of the

Congress. Teachers in the foreign language classrooms in schools and colleges may finally have a solid source of financial support for their field.

Presently, as many faculty realize, funding for foreign language pedagogy is not a clearly defined responsibility of any major federally-funded foundation. The work of the National Endowment for the Humanities tends to focus on the advanced levels of languages, on translation, or on the use of texts in foreign languages as part of education in the humanities. The National Science Foundation and the U.S. Department of Education fund certain carefully prescribed projects related to foreign languages, but in each case, program restrictions can cause distortions in projects designed to develop or test methodologies to enhance foreign language acquisition. Foreign language faculty have only to ask colleagues in ESOL how difficult they find the pursuit of support for research in foreign language pedagogy to realize how little direct funding is available with current resources. A single entity responsible for funding state-of-the-art work in second language learning will give a significant boost to the field.

Adult Use of Foreign Languages

The need for a new National Center for foreign language pedagogy and a National Endowment is particularly important in light of discussions about the importance of adult use of foreign languages in the United States. The notion of "adult use of foreign language" may need some explanation. Looking at the overall picture in the United States, the fact is that few adults can speak second languages unless they are bilinguals from birth. Few professions have demanded foreign language proficiency as a criterion for hiring. Few adults read for pleasure in foreign languages. This situation is destructive to young people's motivation to learn languages, to language faculty's motivation to teach them, and to parents' motivation to encourage real proficiency. Perhaps it is simply true that Americans do not need languages. Perhaps few adults use second languages because so few really have any significant, useful proficiency, oral or otherwise. This is a chicken-and-egg problem.

The notion of "adult use of foreign languages" encourages the redefinition of "adult" and the expansion of specific opportunities for larger numbers of adults to use a second language. Adult means anyone over 18, so all college students fall into this category. The expansion of opportunities includes efforts to reinstate language proficiency for state department, foreign service, and diplomatic work, establish high oral proficiency language requirements for entry into prestigious graduate programs in the professions (see the description of the Lauder Institute below), develop preferential hiring practices by corporations, medical and legal practices, and social service agencies. It also includes the offering of content courses in a range of college disciplines in foreign languages. If more of our school and college students felt that the time and effort they spend to acquire a language would really yield them language proficiency and really remain an advantage in their careers, they would study harder. If language teachers knew that their devoted investments of creative teaching would yield a lifetime of usable knowledge and skills for their students, perhaps they would become less discouraged and work harder at articulation between levels. If parents perceived a pragmatic as well as personal benefit to their children over the long term, it is possible that they would insist on language instruction at earlier stages in the children's education and on better materials; and they would support more opportunities for teachers to study abroad and refresh their skills.

The American tradition in the foreign language field has tended to focus on interrupted sequences of elementary and intermediate language instruction. Here is where the largest number of enrollments occur, and this is where they end as well. We need a whole new look at this system. One that takes the perspective of *outcomes*. What is the outcome for the nation that the profession wants to see from the time, effort, and funding expended for language instruction in the United States? Adult use includes professional and job-related use as well as personal use of language to enjoy traveling and reading. The teaching of youngsters, adolescents, and young adults will benefit greatly from a realistic focus on "adult use."

Of course, "adult use" surveys probably need to be conducted to discover how many adults currently do use foreign languages in their work and—more importantly—how many perceive a need for languages even though they have not developed proficiency. It would be helpful to know how adults could revive their lost language skills. Privately-owned foreign language schools like Berlitz and Inlingua are among the fastest-growing enterprises in the country. It is easy to suspect that a good number of adults must see a need for languages they do not have if these adults and their corporations are willing to pay significant fees for private language instruction, often after work hours. To prepare students for their lives in the twenty-first century, the foreign language profession needs to look at the adult use issue and use it to strengthen the case for language study from kindergarten to graduate school.[2]

Academic Alliance

While both the National Center and the Endowment are in developmental stages and we are rethinking the importance of adult use of foreign languages, collaborative efforts between school and college faculty continue to grow in the Academic Alliance project. In the past five years, the Academic Alliance project has helped to initiate more than 100 collaborative groups of foreign language and literature faculty in the schools and colleges around the country. These groups, modeled after the original county medical societies and county bar associations in the 1890s, now draw school and college faculty together as professional colleagues with a common agenda. Meeting monthly or bi-monthly, faculty in these groups take responsibility together for the equality of teaching and learning in the discipline they share. More than 3,000 faculty throughout the United States are currently engaged in this kind of professional activity. They are reinforcing the work being done at the national, state, and regional meetings. Their monthly contact with each other has served to improve articulation in the curriculum, enrich the range of teaching and testing materials available in the schools and colleges, and ensure better levels of professional engagement among both the faculty and their students.

School and college teachers are creating dynamic learning environments for each other. Some exciting projects include:

• The Ohio Valley Foreign Language Alliance and Ohio University are offering summer language camp and summer institutes for advanced language students to encourage student interest in foreign languages and cultures.

• Since 1982, Michele Shockey, a member of the Santa Clara/San Mateo Collaborative in California, has offered Advanced Placement Seminars for French teachers. A recent seminar had 165 current and future AP teachers at Stanford.

• The theme of the annual fall conference of the Connecticut Council of Language

Teachers in cooperation with the Connecticut Council for the Social Studies was "Foreign Languages and Social Studies: Together We're Better."

• Language Expo '86 presented by the Indiana Foreign Language Cooperative featured workshops on "Developing Foreign Language Proficiency in the Classroom" and "Practical Application of Random Access Videodisk Technology."

• The Greater Boston Collaborative is participating in the College Board's Educational Equality Project Program for School/College Collaboration.

Alliance groups have won the confidence of administrators and government offices:

• Members of the Santa Clara/San Mateo Seminar were named to the California State Foreign Language Advisory Committee which was commissioned to create a new statement and model curriculum standards for foreign language education in California.

• Mary de Lopez of the Albuquerque Language Teachers Association published an article which outlines, step by step, ALTA's successful relationship with the local television and radio stations and with the press.

• The Foreign Language Association of North Dakota received $8,000 from the State Department of Public Instruction to form a North Dakota State Foreign Language Advisory Council to survey the needs of the state.

• ALTA (New Mexico) formed a task force to investigate reinstating the position of state coordinator of modern and classical languages. This was the direct result of recommendations for reform in second language education submitted to the Legislative Educational Reform Committee by ALTA committee members.

• The Ohio Valley Foreign Language Alliance formed a task force to upgrade foreign language instruction. This document which was circulated to local teachers and administrators listed 26 recommendations as a starting point from which students, teachers, and schools can build effective programs of international understanding, cultural awareness, and foreign language proficiency.

When school and college faculty work together, they make a cogent case for funding for the projects they identify.

• Northern Arizona University Collaborative received a federal grant of $57,000 under the Critical Language Program.

• Arkansas Technical University Collaborative received a grant of $40,250 from the Arkansas Department of Higher Education.

• A state-wide network of Alliances in Georgia received $8,967 from the Georgia Endowment for the Humanities.

• Purdue University–Calumet was awarded funding by the Department of Education under Title II.

• The Department of Higher Education renewed a grant of $36,000 to the Northern New Jersey Foreign Language Collaborative.

• The Ohio Valley Foreign Language Alliance has received a grant of $40,000 from the Ohio Board of Regents.

In each issue of *Foreign Language Annals* since October 1984, Academic Alliance groups have reported their activities to their colleagues in the profession. *Collaborare*, the newsletter of the Academic Alliances in Foreign Languages, began in January 1986 when the supervision and development of the language alliances was transferred to the able direction of Ellen Silber at Marymount College.

In fall 1986, the American Association of Higher Education published a monograph describing the Alliance concept of school and college faculty collaboration.[3] This book, supported by a grant from the ARCO Foundation, reaches 6,000 presidents, deans, and educators at all levels. The leadership of foreign language faculty in this movement to create longlasting collaboration between school and college faculty is a credit to our discipline. These publications and the efforts of colleagues throughout the nation have helped to create a positive spirit among language faculty in schools and colleges. These teachers understand that they share common ground; that language instruction needs careful articulation among elementary, intermediate, and advanced levels; and that the study of language cannot easily be separated from the study of culture.

It should be noted incidentally that the leadership shown by foreign language and literature faculty in developing Academic Alliances has had a resonating effect throughout the academic community. There are currently Alliance groups of school and college faculty operating in history and social studies, chemistry, physics, mathematics, and English. School and college faculty collaboration is likely to grow in all disciplines in the future since these groups offer sensible ways for faculty to maintain their own attachment to the discipline and help improve American education cost effectively.[4]

Rockefeller Foundation Fellowships

When the Rockefeller Foundation made a decision to offer its support to school teachers, the existence of the Academic Alliances network attracted the attention of the Foundation's program officers. The Foundation wanted to assure that its program would reach the largest number of teachers possible all over the country and that they would receive support and encouragement in preparing proposals. The result of this interest is the Rockefeller Foundation Fellowships for Foreign Language Teachers in the Schools, a commitment of $1.5 million. This program, administered by Academic Alliances, offers $4,500 summer study fellowships to school teachers of foreign languages. The Alliance groups throughout the country distribute applications and encourage and review proposals. In fact, the Foundation selected the Academic Alliances office as the administrative unit for this project because Academic Alliances speaks to the importance of long term collaboration between school and college faculty in the development of joint communities of inquiry among adults who teach the same discipline. In the first year, 70 Academic Alliance groups across the country served as dissemination points for applications in their geographical areas and also served as initial review panels for the project. These local review panels brought school and college faculty together with community leaders to evaluate proposals and guide teachers in the development of more competitive projects. During the 1986 grant competition, more than 900 applications came from school teachers in all 50 states, the Virgin Islands, and American schools abroad. Faculty in Alliances made an extraordinary effort to recruit applications from a wide range of teachers, none of whom had to be members of Academic Alliance groups in order to participate in the Rockefeller project. In fact, fewer than half of the 900 applications received came from teachers who belong to Academic Alliances groups.

The first group of 95 fellows spent eight weeks of summer study on five continents studying nine languages. Rockefeller Fellows came from small rural schools and large urban institutions. Some joined existing study programs abroad, others created their own study programs. Many returned with videotape and slide presentations to enrich their classrooms. Among the 95 recipients were:

Doris S. Brody
Lincoln High School
Philadelphia, PA

Doris Brody, a French teacher, studied French business and economics at the Chambre de Commerce et d'Industrie de Paris. She then engaged in an internship at Pernod and toured southern France with a member of the French Ministry of Labor to investigate new enterprises at various sites. She has prepared new materials for her students to update their knowledge of modern France.

Diane M. Clawson
Valley Christian School
Missoula, MT

Ms. Clawson studied at a German language institute in Austria before pursuing independent study in Germany while staying with German families. She produced slides and videotapes that will reveal to her students many different life styles and occupations in Germany. She interviewed a detective, a brewsmaster, a baker, a butcher, a former race-car driver, a teacher, a pharmacist, and others. Her materials will be shared with her students and other German teachers.

Sybil J. Gilchrist
Medford (MA) High School

Ms. Gilchrist is a teacher of French, Latin, and Chinese who used the fellowship to improve her proficiency in Mandarin Chinese. She studied in an immersion program at Harvard University that emphasized literature and conversation. She is now able to offer more advanced Chinese courses in her high school.

Elizabeth L. Heimbach
St. Stephen's School
Fairfax, VA

Ms. Heimbach, a Latin teacher, visited Pompeii to research victims of the eruption of Vesuvius and prepare profiles based on the writings of those who witnessed the eruption in 79 A.D. She prepared a ten-unit series of materials for her students, featuring education, entertainment, and animals in Pompeii as well as particular citizens.

Gary M. Thelen
Theodore Roosevelt High School
West Des Moines, LA

Mr. Thelen arranged for independent study in Morocco and Tunisia in order to prepare units on the French-speaking cultures of the Maghreb. He is now familiar with French colonialism in North Africa, the controversy surrounding immigration from the Maghreb into France, and the Muslim culture and will integrate new information into his curriculum.

Two significant elements make the Rockefeller program distinctive. Teachers must show evidence of long term leadership efforts to improve foreign language teaching in their local area. They must offer a clear plan showing how they will share the benefits of their summer study with their fellow teachers of foreign languages. These provisions help assure that leadership and collegiality will be encouraged by the fellowship program.

The Rockefeller Foundation has committed itself to three years of funding for 100 summer study fellowships for high school foreign language teachers. The Foundation believes that school teachers of languages are a critical link in the development of international perspectives and foreign language proficiency for American citizens. The Foundation's intent is to reward and encourage excellence among school teachers of foreign languages. With the additional funding available from the Foundation for summer study abroad, school faculty working together with college faculty have increasing opportunities to develop language proficiency, expertise in the teaching of culture, and a deeper commitment to the significance of foreign languages for America's future.

Other Collaborations

The National Endowment for the Humanities has initiated a collaborative grants program that permits school and college faculty to apply for funding together to enhance their work in their discipline. One such project will bring faculty from University of Wisconsin and school teachers from the state together for a month in a French language institute in summer 1987. At the University of Minnesota–Morris, a program provided funds to develop small foreign language programs which encouraged the creation of a network of college faculty and secondary school teachers in the area. Summer 1986, the New York University Paris immersion program sent 20 teachers to France for intensive language studies. This contemporary French culture immersion also provided studies in history, culture, and social issues. The existence of this grant program should encourage more joint prospects in the future.

School and college faculty collaboration is one kind of collaboration that has already had impact in our field. However, the new environment for language study is also stimulating collaboration among faculty in disciplines related to, but outside of, the foreign language and literature area. For instance, ESOL faculty have long faced many of the same challenges faced by foreign language faculty, although in the past these two groups have rarely benefited from each other's research and experience. The new national agenda recommends that the more highly refined experimental methods in research developed by ESOL specialists be evaluated for their applicability to the foreign language classroom. In the future, teams of foreign language and ESOL faculty will collaborate on projects designed to identify ways to enhance language learning, cope with language loss, increase the development of vocabulary designed for adult use of languages in a range of professions, and develop effective ways to assist adults in maintaining the language proficiency they once achieved in a classroom setting. The research and teaching agendas of foreign language and ESOL faculty are already being brought together in a number of sites. This trend is expected to grow in the future.

Other collaborations lie ahead for the foreign language teacher. For years the field of foreign language has suffered with the prejudices and misunderstandings among teachers who are not native speakers of the target languages taught in our departments. In an excellent analysis of this problem, Elinor Jorden, Distinguished Professor at the new National Center for Foreign Languages at SAIS, The Johns Hopkins University, has not only named these two groups appropriately but has developed a productive way for each group to make a meaningful contribution to the advancement to the national language agenda. Jorden defines two kinds of teachers. The target native teachers are those who are native speakers of the students' native language. By defining two kinds of teachers, target natives and base natives, Jorden articulates a complementary impact each has on the students' learning curve. Base native teachers understand the special linguistic and cultural barriers that students must overcome to achieve proficiency and sensitivity to the new culture. Target native teachers have native language proficiency and firsthand experience in the culture. Together they can help each other to communicate the language and culture to their students and learn from each other as well. She advocates the creation of teaching teams in school and college language departments. She advises that each team be composed of a target native and base native teacher. Teaching teams would share each other's students, visit each other's classes, develop together meaningful exercises and testing, and divide responsibility for the teaching of culture according to their different and complementary expertise. By outlining how to overcome the long-accepted uneasiness or sometimes even animosity between these two kinds of foreign language teachers, Jorden indicates how language learning itself can advance using the team approach. This idea, long overdue, can be adopted in both schools and in colleges with little disturbance in staffing patterns but with great potential for improved utilization of skills and resources. The collaboration of target and base native faculty can have an extraordinary impact on the development of language skills in the United States.[5]

The challenge of the coming years will also necessitate collaboration among different kinds of institutions. Some collaborations, like the consortium that brings Brigham Young University, the University of Iowa, Middlebury College, and MIT together, are designed to enhance the utilization of technology for the benefit of language learning. This consortium brings the strengths of each institution in computer technology, audio and video materials development, and language learning to bear on the production of improved language teaching methods. Faculty engaged in the consortium are experimenting with new software and videodiscs and expect to accelerate both the rate and level of language learning per hour of instruction. The field stands to benefit considerably from the collaborative efforts of the faculty and students engaged in this consortium.

The Ivy Consortium offers another kind of collaboration. The Ivy League institutions joined by Stanford, MIT, and the University of Chicago have formed a consortium whose objective is to improve the study of foreign languages on their campuses. These leadership institutions are in a position to attract the attention of parents, school administrators, and both government and academic leaders. We all remember when colleges, particularly eminent institutions, dropped their language requirements, the resonance of these decisions was felt through the academic enterprise. As the Ivy Consortium puts new stress on the importance of foreign language study, other colleges, school systems, parents, and students throughout the nation will pay attention.

Graduate language departments, both in the foreign language field and outside, have recently taken a new look at how they can collaborate to better prepare for the internationalized life of the year 2000. During an NEH-sponsored conference at the University of Virginia, 50 members of the largest Ph.D.-granting departments in the foreign language and literature field met to review their programs and suggest new directions for the future. These institutions, under the leadership of Richard Brod, recognized the importance of preparing the next generation of faculty to teach language, literature, and culture well; to supervise language instruction in major institutions; and to prepare a larger number of language-proficient adults for careers in the year 2000. While the importance of the study of literature was emphasized, frequent reference was made to the importance of preparing students to deal with a range of other content areas in foreign languages.[6]

As collaborations have grown among graduate departments, such as those attending the University of Virginia conference, so have collaborations grown between graduate schools and professional schools. In the last ten years, several graduate management programs have developed opportunities for students heading toward international management to acquire advanced language skills. The first such program, the Master's in International Business Studies at the University of South Carolina, offers students six-month internships overseas as part of an extensive language study program. The program helps assure that students develop advanced language skills and an understanding of the foreign business environment before they complete their management studies in American degrees.

The Lauder Institute

In 1983, the Joseph H. Lauder Institute of Management and International Studies began at the University of Pennsylvania. The 50 new students accepted into this two-year program each year receive the MBA from the Wharton School and the MA in International Studies from the School of Arts and Sciences at Penn. Entry requirements for the joint degree program include an advanced level of foreign language proficiency as indicated by an oral proficiency test given by an ACTFL certified tester in one of nine foreign languages: Chinese, French, German, Hindi, Japanese, Portuguese, Russian, Spanish, and English for foreign students. The program's high language requirements match the high quantitative requirements expected of candidates for entry into the Wharton School. Before graduation from the 24-month program, students must achieve a superior level on the oral proficiency test. These requirements also mean that currently a large number of undergraduates from the American colleges are not adequately prepared for admissions. The Institute intends to send a message to high schools, undergraduate colleges, students, and parents. This message clearly states that achieving advanced-level language proficiency is an undergraduate task and that graduate work involves the move from advanced to superior levels of language proficiency. In the same way, algebra, trigonometry, and calculus are high school and undergraduate level work in math. Graduate level work in the management disciplines builds on this important base. The Lauder Institute's graduate level work in both languages and the management disciplines should prepare a bright and highly motivated person to function effectively and comfortably as an international manager. The move from advanced to superior levels of language proficiency assures that this manager will communicate appropriately as a professional in the foreign environment. Lauder students take an oral proficiency test in their language five times during their 24-month course of study.[7]

Lauder Fellows' language and cultural perspectives curriculum shows the importance of collaboration among language faculty and those in history, anthropology, sociology, economics, and the other social sciences. Lectures each week from the faculty provide some of the source material for the part of the course dedicated to building language skills. Students collaborate with the faculty by developing readers in each of the foreign languages for each of the required courses in the Wharton MBA core program. These anthologies provide students with important perspectives from abroad on the strategies and structures they study in their management coursework. The Exxon Education Foundation provided the Institute a grant to develop these readers. Lauder students also spend two summers abroad. They spend eight weeks in intensive study their first summer and 12 weeks working in a corporate environment where they use their second language daily during their second summer.

The success of these students can only encourage more young students to take second language courses seriously. It can only encourage the corporate sector to believe that American education can produce linguistically and culturally competent adults — a feat we have not achieved regularly in the past in graduate management programs.

The enthusiastic support of corporate leaders for these new efforts in international management studies is encouraging additional institutions to undertake the development of similar programs. For instance, Drexel University has developed an undergraduate analog of the Lauder Institute for its students in international studies for management. In each new program, a board of advisors composed of academic and corporate leaders can help assure that the aims of both sectors will be met and yield good results for the students who are preparing for their careers in international management.

Conclusion

The foreign language teacher is a key factor in the internationalization of American education. The collaborative efforts at many levels throughout the nation will assure that work of language teachers will not go unappreciated or unrecognized. This work must occur in a context that supports the importance of the task undertaken in the language classroom and places that work in the context of the adult use of the second language for a range of different personal and professional reasons.

Notes

1 International agenda policy papers are available in the May 1987 issue of the *Annals* of the American Academy of Political and Social Science.

2 The notion of adult use was discussed in detail at the Aspen conference and is an important concept in the national agenda for foreign languages.

3 To receive a free copy of this monograph, write to Academic Alliances, 210 Logan Hall, CGS, University of Pennsylvania, Philadelphia, PA 19104-6384. For directions on how to enter the Academic Alliance project, write the same address for application materials or call 215-898-3112.

4 For further information on starting an Alliance in your area, please write to Academic Alliances, 210 Logan Hall, CGS, University of Pennsylvania, Philadelphia, PA 19104-6384.

5 *Conference Report: New Priorities for the Teaching and Learning of Asian Languages*, October 2, 1981, East Asia Program, The Wilson Center, Smithsonian Institution Building, Washington, DC 20560. Elinor Jorden, "Japanese Language Teaching: Whence, Where, and Whither." Ronald Walton, "Conflicting Paradigms in Foreign Language Education: Rethinking."

6 A review of some of the papers given at that conference can be found in the *ADFL Bulletin*, Spring 1986.

7 For further information on the design of the foreign language program as well as the general Lauder program, please write Joseph H. Lauder Institute of Management and International Studies, University of Pennsylvania, 3620 Locust Walk, Philadelphia, PA 19104. For further information on the MIBS program, write MIBS, University of South Carolina, Columbia, SC 29208.

A recent publication edited by Samia Spencer, *Foreign Language and International Trade: A Global Perspective*, contains a useful set of essays from government, corporate, and academic leaders focused on the importance of preparing American students to compete more effectively in international trade.

HUMPHREY TONKIN was appointed President of Potsdam College of SUNY in May 1983 by the State University of New York Board of Trustees and assumed direction of the College on September 1, 1983. Mr. Tonkin came to Potsdam from Philadelphia where he was Professor of English, Coordinator of International Programs and Master of Stouffer College House at the University of Pennsylvania. He joined that institution in 1966 as Assistant Professor of English where his administrative career included the positions of Director of Freshman English and Vice-Provost for Undergraduate Studies. He received the Lindback Award for Distinguished Teaching in 1970 and was named a Guggenheim Fellow in 1974.

Mr. Tonkin has lectured on English literature, languages, and international studies at universities in many parts of the world, and in 1980–81 was Visiting Professor of English and Comparative Literature at Columbia University.

The author of numerous books, monographs, and articles, he is best known for three diverse publications: *The World in the Curriculum: Curricular Strategies for the 21st Century*, co-authored with his wife, Jane Edwards (1981); *Esperanto and International Language Problems: A Research Bibliography* (1977); and *Spenser's Courteous Pastoral: Book Six of the Faerie Queene* (1972). He is a bibliographer for the Modern Language Association and Managing Editor of the journal *Language Problems and Language Planning*.

An active advocate of international cooperation and international studies, Mr. Tonkin was elected President of the Universal Esperanto Association (UEA) in August 1986 and serves as representative of that association at the United Nations. He also serves on the boards of the Council for the International Exchange of Scholars (which administers the Fulbright Program) and Global Perspectives in Education. He chairs the board of the Center for Research and Documentation on World Language Problems and is a former president of the Spenser Society.

Mr. Tonkin holds the baccalaureate and master's degrees from St. John's College, Cambridge University, and the A.M. and the Ph.D. degrees from Harvard University.

Humphrey Tonkin

Grassroots and Treetops: Collaboration in Post-secondary Language Programs

Introduction

A little less than ten years ago, when the work of the President's Commission on Foreign Language and International Studies was in full swing, my colleagues and I, at the university with which I was then associated, called a conference. It was an internal affair for our own faculty members and administrators, and it was convened to formulate the university's position on the matters under consideration by the Commission. We were worried that no one would come. We were particularly worried that foreign languages would be underrepresented. After all, political scientists and economists who concerned themselves at all with the larger world could readily identify themselves with the concept of international studies; but the people in the foreign language departments, though they received notices of the conference, tended not to see themselves as a part of the international studies community. For them, the designation "foreign languages and international studies" would seem to refer to area studies specialists and the like, not to teachers of Spanish or French or German.

In the event, we did better than we expected. Our professors of Gujarati and Tibetan and Arabic were there in force, to be sure, but so were the teachers of the more widely taught languages. This was the first time that many of them had sat down with their colleagues in the social sciences to discuss common problems — or, to put the matter more precisely, to talk about whether they might conceivably have some problems in common. By the time the conference was over, some of these problems had indeed been defined; and, at the very least, there was a feeling that specialists in international studies and specialists in foreign languages should make common cause, both to convince their colleagues of the importance of the international dimension of higher education and also to persuade the public and the politicians to pay greater attention to the preparation of our citizens for life in an interdependent world.

The conference was not without its unsettling moments. So monolingual is the environment of many of our social scientists that it was hard for them to confront the fact that Foucault actually wrote in French, or that Levi-Strauss was not an honorary American, or that our understanding of Marx or Hegel might be vitiated by linguistic inexactitude as their terminology was translated from German into English. Perhaps the worst moment came when one of our foreign-born language teachers rose to his feet and solemnly proposed that Congress pass a law requiring compulsory language study in all United States schools beginning in the first grade. He seemed reluctant to concede that the American educational system was not a product of national government and could not be altered at will by a determined legislature in Washington. His views were not so very different from those of many of his foreign language colleagues, who had never thought very seriously about the politics of foreign language study or about strategies for raising the consciousness of Americans about global affairs.

In less than ten years, a veritable revolution has taken place. Mainstream foreign language teachers, representing the vast bulk of foreign language enrollments across the country, have organized themselves into a formidable lobby, both in Washington and in the states. Language study has reappeared on the national agenda, and there is hardly a state in the Union that has not begun to confront the question of improving instruction in foreign languages in its schools (Draper, 1984). Organizations like the Joint National Committee for Languages (JNCL) have sprung up to champion the cause, and even such organizations as the Modern Language Association and the American Council on the Teaching of Foreign Languages, two of the organizations that created the JNCL, have become politically active on behalf of foreign language study.

At that conference, in the late 1970s, it was already evident that the sap was stirring. Years of falling enrollments had had their effect. The bewilderment that accompanied that decline was being replaced by a sense that concrete action was needed. The teachers of European languages took their cue from the area studies specialists, whose powerful lobbying efforts, geared to articulation of the national interest, had, ever since the National Defense Education Act in the late 1950s, brought them attention and financial support from lawmakers in Washington (Lambert, 1973, 1980). In short, a much larger collaborative effort was evolving that would soon involve many teachers who had never before thought about the national interest in languages or the need to lobby for funds.

Today, the foreign language teacher in the average United States college or university is far more likely to be aware of political imperatives than ten years ago. While the message has still to reach many of our colleagues in its full force, the need to serve as advocates for foreign language study, to work with colleagues in other disciplines, to change the focus and the substance of instruction—this is widely recognized in the profession. There is, however, still much to be done. Merely recognizing that foreign language teachers and international studies specialists are allies is not at all the same thing as recognizing that they have intellectual ground in common. Understanding that administrators and fellow faculty members must be convinced of the value of foreign language study, or that public support must be built, is not the same thing as actually doing the convincing or building the support. Nor is it enough merely to recognize that the curriculum must change or teaching methods be altered. Practical paths to the achievement of these ends must be discovered. The pages that follow will be devoted to an examination of what those paths might be. They are heavily indebted to others who have examined this topic before me—in the pages of the *ADFL Bulletin*, *Foreign Language Annals*, and elsewhere, and particularly to Gaudiani and Herron (1984), the best and most detailed discussion of the subject to date (see also Phillips, 1981; Tonkin and Edwards, 1981).

The Fundamentals of Language

LANGUAGE AND SOCIETY

At the risk of beginning my discussion with a topic seemingly remote from the matter at hand, or, more precisely, a topic that we might expect to take for granted, I want to begin by raising some questions about our understanding of what language is, since only if we understand its nature can we effectively integrate it into a curriculum. Most language teachers have entered the profession through training in departments of language and literature, whose methods and curriculum derive ultimately from the study of the classical languages and whose assumptions about language are diachronic and historically-based. This training is very different from a training in linguistics, a discipline which has essentially overcome, or outlived, its philological origins and whose approach to language is synchronic and comparative, and, to an increasing degree, interdisciplinary. I will suggest that we must rediscover this link with linguistics, a link which only the teachers of English to Speakers of Other Languages have made use of to any appreciable extent. Teachers of ESOL, faced with a very practical and immediate task and less constrained by received academic assumptions about language teaching, have sought help wherever they can find it; most departments of foreign languages, however, have remained faithful to their academic origins and have given relatively little attention to revolutionary new developments in sociolinguistics or to the whole question of the social and political implications of language. It is here, in my view, that the language teacher of the future must begin. Language teaching should not be conceived of as the passing on of an academic tradition (though that may be one of its by-products) but as a highly practical pursuit, whose aim is proficiency and utility. At the same time, language teaching in a liberal arts context should help the student to understand what language is and how it works. Our first aim, then, is achievement—crossing the threshold of utility so that the newly acquired language can be put to practical use. Our second aim is to use the new language to broaden the students' view of the world and understanding of the nature of language itself.

Language is, first and foremost, a social and political phenomenon, an economic and cultural reality that is all around us. The study of language is an essential element in the undergraduate curriculum not because it would be nice to be able to read a foreign literature in the original or gain a passing acquaintance with a foreign culture but because the world of which we are a part is a multilingual world. Language is the key to an understanding of that world. We cannot learn to speak all languages, or even all of the most important; but we can learn how to learn, and we can discover how to read other cultures. Locked in the prison-house of our own language, even though it may be widely spoken across the world, we are intellectually and culturally impoverished—and there is some indication that we may be economically impoverished as well.

Born of the human need to communicate, language is also a mode of behavior, a social phenomenon. Different communities use different linguistic forms, and the sum of linguistic behavior in a given community constitutes that community's language. Different subsets of that behavior may carry more or less prestige and may be linked with particular power structures in the community (Bernstein, 1971). They may be used for mass communication or carry some legal or official status. Where such characteristics come together, we recognize the existence of a standard language. Since it is normally the purpose of the language teacher to teach the forms of language behavior in a given community that will allow the student to identify with the most influential sections of the population, the language teacher is primarily interested in standard language. In some instances, for example Spanish and English, different forms of standard language prevail in different geographical areas and choosing the right one to teach may pose a problem.

LANGUAGE AND POLITICS

Language is a part of the geopolitical system. Possession of a particular language may define (and be defined by) the situation of a given country on the world scene. When the British came to Africa in the nineteenth century, they brought English with them. Today, even though the British Empire has been dismantled, English remains the official language of government in most countries that were once part of the Empire, even though in some countries only a fraction of the population may be capable of using it. In imperial days, English was the language of literacy, the language of the colonial bureaucracy. Since the countries of Africa were largely artificial creations, carved out of the continent without regard to ethnic and linguistic boundaries, these countries generally lack a single widely spoken language of their own. Countries like Nigeria or Sierra Leone or Zaire may have as many as a hundred languages within their borders and even the elites of those countries may have no indigenous languages in common. Hence they must retain English or French if they are to maintain themselves as countries. As a result, Nigeria and Sierra Leone remain firmly within the British orbit. Zaire, formerly linked with Belgium, retains many of those links. Significantly, when Nigeria tried some years ago to reform its political system, it flirted with the American system of government. As for Zaire, after Belgium the strongest foreign influence comes from France. In short, the linguistic link between Africa and Europe remains strong, even in the post-colonial era. Economic and political ties follow, and are reinforced by, the official languages of the countries in question. Students from Senegal study in France; those from Ghana or Nigeria gravitate to Britain and the United States.

In those former colonies where the language of the mother country has largely disappeared, such as Indonesia, where Dutch is little used, there was a reasonably high degree of linguistic unity before the colonists arrived. In some countries, such as the Philippines, identification with a particular language carries political significance. Thus the rebels in that country stress Pilipino to the exclusion of English; the ruling party (and its predecessor the Marcos regime) is identified with the learning and use of English and with friendship for the United States (Tollefson, 1986).

ENGLISH AS A WORLD LANGUAGE

Over the past twenty or thirty years, the situation of English in the world has undergone a profound change (Fishman, Cooper, and Conrad, 1977). Today, English is far and away the most studied foreign language in the world. In all of Western Europe, only in Britain and Ireland does French remain the most popular foreign language (though it remains relatively strong in Italy) (Szepe, 1980). In Eastern Europe, English has largely displaced Russian as the most widely studied language, though French retains some status in Romania and Russian in Bulgaria. English is widely taught in Japan and is increasing in popularity in China. In these countries, English is regarded not only as the language of what is, in effect, an international popular culture, but also as a route to social and economic influence. It is also recognized as the language of technology, of science, of education.

English has reached this position with astounding rapidity. Essentially the language of a few off-shore European islands in the sixteenth and seventeenth centuries (when Italian and French were the languages of the elite and Dutch dominated commerce), English spread across the world in the eighteenth and nineteenth centuries. Only in 1919, with the Conference of Versailles and subsequently the establishment of the League of Nations, did it directly challenge French as the language of international diplomacy. When the United Nations was founded in 1945, English and French were the first working languages (there were three additional "official" languages), but between then and 1973 they were joined by Russian, Spanish, Chinese, and Arabic (Humblet, 1984). German enjoys some official status at the United Nations (Paqué, 1983) and such languages as Portuguese, Japanese, Indonesian, and Hindi-Urdu are waiting, in various degrees of readiness, in the wings. The European Community is up to nine languages, all enjoying equal status (Patterson, 1982). The United Nations, of course, has three writing systems among its six languages; the European Community has two.

The proliferation of languages at the United Nations or in the European Community would seem to suggest that English is losing its authority as a means of international communication. This is not entirely so. Because the decisions of the European Parliament have legal status in the member countries, the European Community is obliged to use all the official languages of its members (Patterson, 1982). As for the United Nations, power relationships have been the major determinants of the languages used. It is no accident that the languages of the United Nations are largely the languages of the victorious allies in 1945, nor is it an accident that Arabic was added at the height of the oil crisis. At stake in the United Nations is not communication, but *privileged* communication. The owners of the languages used at the United Nations enjoy increased prestige and increased convenience, and they are able to intervene more effectively in this organization's affairs, thereby reinforcing their positions of power.

An English-speaking United Nations (if English were the chosen language) would be politically very different from the current organization: all non-English-speaking countries would be pushed onto the political defensive (and a kind of communicative defensive too), because language is power, and command of the means of linguistic expression is power. For these reasons, the likelihood of an officially monolingual United Nations seems remote indeed, and the idea is probably inadvisable as well.

LANGUAGE POLICY

Even as English consolidates its position in other areas of world affairs, and even as it continues to be used as a language of government, the former colonial powers are observing varying degrees of decline in the knowledge of English within their borders. This is an ongoing problem in India, where English and Hindi are the languages of the central government, and in Nigeria (Jolly and Robertson, 1985). In these highly multilingual countries, the making of particular language choices (which languages will be used in which political and public institutions, which languages will be languages of instruction at which levels, which languages will be used for which forms of mass communications) may well determine the entire political and economic direction of the country (Fishman, Ferguson, and Das Gupta, 1968). Hence the formulation of language policy is utterly central among national concerns (Weinstein, 1983). It is easy for those of us in the United States to call for the creation of democratic institutions in Third World countries, but that may be more difficult to achieve in a country where only five percent of the population speaks the language of government and hence only five percent is in practice eligible to run for public office. Indeed, it may well be that without some form of language planning and language standardization no reasonably representative system of government can be developed at all. We look askance at the efforts of Quebec or France to legislate language use, little realizing that in some parts of the world radical realignment of languages is going on of necessity (Kennedy, 1983, 1985; Cobarrubias and Fishman, 1983; Eastman, 1983).

Even in Europe and North America language policy has emerged as a serious issue. The situation of Spanish in the United States highlights for us the problem of reconciling individual rights with the larger public interest as Spanish speakers insist on access to social services in their own language; and others call on them to assimilate, regardless of the pain involved and the potential cultural deracination. In some parts of the world — Britain and France for example — entire languages are threatened with extinction (Trudgill, 1984, Laponce, 1984, p. 192). In other cases, linguistic links are used to bolster or blunt territorial claims. Thus the Bulgarians maintain that the Macedonians speak a version of Bulgarian while the Yugoslavs insist that it is Macedonian, and the Greeks refuse to recognize the existence of the Macedonian language within their borders at all. Even the definition of what constitutes a language may be fraught with political meaning. Is Friulian "just a dialect" of Italian, is Occitan "just a dialect" of French, or are they full-blown languages, potentially able to make claims on the constitution and institutions of their countries? The question is not linguistic but political, and linguists are often ill equipped to offer answers.

It is clear, then, that language can be used as a means of discriminating against particular groups of people, and is often so used (Calvet, 1974, Laponce, 1984). A simple change in the language law can disenfranchise entire sections of the population, as Spanish speakers in Dade County, Florida, discovered a few years ago. Language is routinely mentioned in international documents, such as the United Nations Charter and the Universal Declaration of Human Rights, along with such factors as race, religion, gender, and national origin, as one of the specific exclusions in the equal treatment of all people. However, language is different from some of these other factors in that it lies at the heart of communication itself: one cannot simply ignore a person's linguistic characteristics in the same way as one can ignore race or gender. Hence the application of language rights must always involve compromise, and honest people may differ on where the line between individual rights and the common good should be drawn.

LANGUAGE LEARNING IN THE UNITED STATES

Given the influence of English on the world scene, our attitude to language learning in the United States tends, at the very least, to be ambivalent. Do we really need foreign languages? Does not most of the world speak English? In reality, of course, some 85 percent of the world's population does not speak English — though that percentage is declining. (Statistics on language knowledge, especially when they go beyond native languages, are massively inexact and should be handled with caution.) Given the large numbers of non-speakers of English, it would seem, at the very least, prudent to learn other languages.

But the issue is not as simple as that. Two additional factors, one negative and the other positive, need to be taken into consideration. On the negative side, the more the United States uses other languages, the less the incentive for speakers of other languages to learn English. This is the argument of those who would have English declared the official language of the United States; it is also a powerful argument for our insisting on the use of English in international affairs. It was at the point when the Soviet Union began to use English in international conferences that the influence of Russian on the international scene went into sharp decline. Similar refusals on the part of the French have kept French alive as an international force; and this linguistic pride accounts, at least in part, for the success of French in Quebec. Without the support of metropolitan France it is arguable whether the language policies of Quebec could have been conceived, let alone applied (Weinstein, 1976).

However, our assumption that if a foreign country has developed a capability in English, English will serve as a means of communication with it, does not automatically follow. If I am trying to sell to the Japanese, I may well be better off using Japanese to do so, because I thereby demonstrate my willingness to accommodate myself to them, rather than the other way around (Hoegl, 1986, p. 285). In this context, then, mediation between language groups is not as easy as it might have seemed. To work in such an environment, I must either purchase expertise in Japanese or use the language teacher to cultivate such expertise in myself.

BRIDGING THE LANGUAGE GAP

But language teaching is not the only means of mediating between language groups. Translators and interpreters are in effect human switching mechanisms, professionals who convert one linguistic code to another. Translation and interpretation involve a high level of skill and, as we know, are very expensive. Interpreters between certain languages are also very difficult to find: the United Nations continues to have trouble with Arabic and Chinese in this regard, and the European Community faced a major training problem when Greek was introduced. Interpreters and translators are assisted by a growing array of electronic devices. The creation of closed interpretation circuits made simultaneous interpretation possible in the 1940s, and cordless systems have now expanded and simplified procedures. Translators are increasingly assisted by computerized terminology banks and by advanced word processing systems. Machine-assisted translation systems are increasingly employed in international organizations, such as the Pan-American Health Organization, and by some governments (the Canadian, for example). Such systems produce rough machine translations, often from pre-edited texts, which can then be polished by final editing. Some six or seven wholly automated systems are currently also under development, normally using some form of "black-box language" as a bridge between input and output languages. One of these systems uses a modified form of Esperanto (Witkam, 1983). While their designers try to avoid making the grand promises of the advocates of machine translation 30 years ago, encouraging progress is being made. Ultimately, as systems of speech recognition and voice synthesis become more sophisticated there is even a possibility that automated interpretation systems might come into being.

Esperanto merits a word of attention here. It, too, was designed in 1887 to serve as a mediating language. It is relatively easy to learn, having a regular structure and an easily mastered system of word building, and it makes communication possible not just with a single foreign culture but with people from any country or language group. Hundreds of thousands of people use it today, despite occasional declarations by uninformed linguists that it cannot possibly work. While the language has yet to be widely adopted by international organizations or businesses, it is quite frequently used as an introduction to language study and can prove an admirable means of teaching students how a language works (Forster, 1982; Tonkin, 1979).

LANGUAGE AND THE WORLD VIEW

These observations tell us, then, that language is a social institution tightly bound up with other social institutions. The language that a particular culture uses, and the way that that society uses this language, is an important indicator of that society's social organization. Not to be aware of such matters is to miss an essential element in language study.

Despite the value of literary study, one of the greatest handicaps of the language teaching faculties in colleges and universities, at least in the European languages, is the nature of their training. Even the perturbations and new directions in language study over the past ten years or so have done little to redirect doctoral programs — themselves in the hands of literary specialists — away from an exclusive focus on literature, nor is the often meager training in linguistics that doctoral students receive sufficiently broadly based. As a consequence, students leaving the university with a Ph.D. find that much of their training has little bearing on the classroom instruction in which they spend the greater part of their time. Indeed, their experience of classroom instruction before receipt of the doctorate may well have taken place with relatively little guidance or assistance. While it is true that in most fields there is something of a gap between research interests and teaching responsibilities (mathematics comes to mind in this connection, as do the natural sciences), we are currently witnessing a discontinuity in doctoral programs for future language teachers that is almost laughable. "Traditional literary curricula," writes Jacques M. Laroche in a recent article (1985), "are no longer revered as the ultimate consecration for the language major, and many departments are desperately seeking realistic course topics likely to attract respectable enrollments." More to the point, faculty members are desperately seeking to retool, to become acquainted with disciplines for which they have not been trained, and to acquire skills that were not a part of their preparation for teaching.

Most college teachers of foreign languages — indeed teachers of foreign languages at all levels — identify with high culture, with normative and standard language use, with the metropolis. While many come to discover the complexity and variety of the societies whose languages they profess, the thrust of their knowledge and loyalties is centripetal rather than centrifugal: they are in effect paid to produce students who look and sound as much as possible like well educated and prosperous citizens of the countries whose language they speak. That is, after all, part of the purpose of language learning: to socialize the student into another culture.

Without wishing to deny or belittle the importance of this process, we must remember that language study has other aims as well. While we would surely agree that the primary purpose of college and university language teaching is to make students proficient in the language in question, and familiar with its culture and society, language study should also provide students with a view of the world through the eyes of another society or culture. It is not only the student's acquaintance with another culture that matters, but also (and beyond this) the way in which the experience of learning about it forces the student to reevaluate his or her understanding of reality. The student sees his or her own culture with new eyes, not only by learning about the nature of signs (learning a second language teaches us about the relativity of language and about what is or is not transferable from one language to another) but also by standing outside himself or herself and testing received values. In this sense, language teaching is a profoundly subversive activity, since it questions the very processes of socialization that have formed the student in his or her own culture and society.

Ideally this subversion will spill over into the other areas that the student studies. The good language teacher does not teach the language in a vacuum; students should be encouraged to find points of contact between the language they are learning (or, rather, the new society that they are entering) and their own interests. The emphasis in the language classroom should, then, fall not simply on constriction (normative speech, standard forms, metropolitan usages) but also on expansion. A language should be an entrée to a world view. Thus the student's acquaintance with the new culture should not be limited to the study of literature. Very possibly, indeed, literature should not be the primary concern. Nor should the student be confined within the boundaries of metropolitan manifestations of the culture, but should venture out into the provinces and beyond the home country where appropriate. And this is not a plea for Belgian studies or Swiss studies only, but for exploration of the relationship between standard French and Creole or study of the way in which French culture has or has not shaped everyday life in Senegal (Ogden, 1981). It is not simply a plea for attention to Mexico or Argentina, but for examination of the relationship between Spanish and Guaraní in Paraguay or Spanish-speaking and indigenous cultures in Guatemala. The student should make use of the language to study about the world. French views of the Soviet Union are as much a part of understanding French culture as learning how to use the Métro—and, of course, by studying what the French think about the Soviet Union the student will also learn about the Soviet Union. Language study that leads only to the replacement of one ethnocentrism with a second has failed in its primary purpose: the expansion of our intellectual horizons to embrace the larger world.

The Compleat Foreign Language Professor

THE LANGUAGE TEACHER AS STUDENT OF SOCIETY

Power, international politics, economics, human rights—language touches all of these issues and many more besides. While the study of literature and history has an important part in the study of language, it is only one of many approaches to the phenomenon of language. Ideally, the language teacher will have some acquaintance with them all. The language teacher will know how language relates to communications technology (the failure of communications specialists and language specialists to communicate is one of the great intellectual discontinuities of our time), and how human beings use technology to overcome language differences. The language teacher will understand something of the relative standing and influence of the languages of the world—where they are spoken and by whom—and will not ignore the question of the role of English in the world and how that role is changing (Fishman, Cooper, and Conrad, 1977).

While all of this may seem something of a tall order—an impossible task for the teacher brought up on Lope de Vega or Balzac—the topics to which I have been referring are the daily concern of the sociolinguist and the language planner. What I am in effect suggesting is that the divorce between the study of language and the study of linguistics must be ended, and the concerns of the modern student of linguistics must inform the language classroom. We have left to linguistics the synchronic exploration of language, the exploration of non-standard language, and psychological and sociological analysis of linguistic phenomena. We must reclaim this territory. The student of linguistics may ask what language is; for the most part the language teacher merely teaches it without asking this most essential of questions. Language teaching, in short, should not be the exclusive territory of the humanist. The effective language teacher, or the effective language teaching program, should bring the humanities and the social sciences together.

Trained in Racine and *racines* and in a *passé* all too *composé*, the foreign language professor may feel somewhat depressed by the foregoing. We have suggested that the teacher must have a more sophisticated understanding of the role of language than most of our teachers have. We have also suggested that the language teacher have some understanding of the social sciences. There are few better ways of preparing to teach the context of languages than by studying cultural anthropology or learning about the global political economy. This is not to suggest that social scientists understand the importance of language in this context and language teachers do not. On the contrary, social scientists, many of them deficient in language knowledge, may themselves never have broken out of the cocoon of their own language, and may be ill at ease dealing with the role of language. In this respect, of course, the cultural anthropologist is likely to do better than the economist or the political scientist.

ORGANIZATIONS

We shall go on to discuss how the foreign language teacher can work with others to create the support structures that are needed to teach language in this broad and integrated way. But collaboration with others must also involve an element of self-help. There are no substitutes for being involved in professional organizations, subscribing to and *reading* journals, attending conferences, participating in seminars and workshops. These professional organizations should not be too narrowly defined. The Modern Language Association, for example, is more than an organization of literary scholars. Under its umbrella the Association of Departments of Foreign Languages raises questions and offers assistance in the area of language pedagogy and effective organization for foreign language teaching. So do the professional organizations for teachers of particular languages. The American Council on the Teaching of Foreign Languages concentrates particularly on language pedagogy, much of it appropriate to language teaching at all levels. (The effective language professor, of course, will have some acquaintance with elementary and secondary school concerns since many of his or her students may eventually teach at these levels.)

Organizations like the ADFL and ACTFL will also help to keep the language professor informed about "political" developments in the field: new legislation in Washington relevant to language teaching, reports on the situation of languages across the nation, new developments in the individual states, new opportunities for participation in activities related to foreign languages.

But the professor's attention should not be confined to organizations specifically concerned with language learning. Great benefit could be derived from attendance at a conference of the International Studies Association, for example — an organization whose broad umbrella covers everything from classic political science, through generalists concerned with global studies, to various fringe groups associated with social action through nongovernmental organizations. While there is little discussion of language at ISA conventions, the language teacher can learn much about the context of languages by participation, and perhaps also do something to remind social scientists of the importance of the linguistic dimension of their work. While ISA's publications are less useful to the language teacher, the publications of Global Perspectives in Education, an organization that concentrates primarily on global studies in the public schools, are excellent. They include bibliographies on various world and regional issues — particularly on teaching about such issues — and a newsletter that is full of information on publications, conferences, and other new developments in the field. GPE itself organizes conferences from time to time.

If organizations for teachers of specific languages are important, so, too, are area-specific organizations, like the Asia Society, which produces good teaching materials, many of them relevant to language teaching, and various organizations dealing with Latin America and with Africa. We cannot emphasize too strongly that the effective language teacher should be knowledgeable about the world as a whole, and should be able to guide students in the direction of their interests.

JOURNALS

Earlier we discussed other means of overcoming language barriers than conventional foreign language teaching, and we stressed the social and political role of language. Keeping up with journals in these fields is important. We should have some understanding, for example, of developments in machine translation, or in the general area of interpretation and translation — not necessarily from a technical point of view, of course. We should also be aware of developments in the commercial use of language — the language of business, in short. The field of language planning and language policy has an important bearing on that of language teaching, and there are journals in these areas too. The British publication *Language Monthly* comes closest to offering a general view of language in the marketplace, while such journals as *Language in Society, Language Problems and Language Planning*, and *Multilingua* offer an overview of policy and planning. The *Language Planning Newsletter* is currently in abeyance but will soon appear again on a regular basis.

As for materials on language pedagogy, the language teacher will require less guidance here, though *Foreign Language Annals* and the *Modern Language Journal* should under no circumstances be ignored. Particular attention should be paid to the document system ERIC, which offers a large range of papers on language and language teaching and is also a good repository for our own papers and teaching materials that we may wish to share with others.

SELF-HELP AND SHARING

Of course, it is not necessary to join all of these organizations, or to subscribe to every journal. Responsibilities, and materials, can be shared among colleagues, and the college library can supplement these resources (see below). Every teacher should surely read newspapers or magazines in his or her language on a regular basis. They might include materials from Quebec or Spanish-language publications produced in the United States, as well as materials from Europe or Latin America. Such materials are not difficult to obtain, though librarians may need help in identifying sources for foreign language publications.

The language professor must also be willing to participate in conferences and seminars in or on foreign languages. The pages of newsletters and journals published by professional organizations are full of details of such opportunities. It is also, of course, possible to organize activities for one's colleagues at the local or regional level if such activities do not already exist. Such contact with colleagues from other institutions is extremely important, especially in a field in which pedagogical methods play so crucial a role and are changing so rapidly.

A certain measure of mobility, then, and a willingness to invest in a professional library—these seem essential to the compleat language professor. Equally essential is a willingness to share resources with colleagues and to set up mechanisms for the collective sharing of information. Uninformed emotional support for language study is of little utility in the environment of today's campus; the effective professor should be in dispassionate possession of the facts. Sharing, furthermore, should go beyond colleagues in languages. It is particularly important to pass interesting or relevant materials on to department chairs, deans, and other senior administrators, so that they too will respond to foreign language issues not emotionally but with solid information.

Teachers can change nothing simply by thinking about it. They must speak out and speak up, follow through and follow up. Specifically, after reading an article, listening to a speaker, or participating in a worthwhile professional activity, they should share their ideas with the speaker, author, or organizer—preferably in writing—to extend the process of learning and establish a dialogue. If teachers of language cannot use language effectively, who can? The compleat language professor must be diplomat and advocate—a generalist who can meet others halfway and a specialist who knows the facts about the field.

Cooperation in International Studies

One cannot help wondering how many people with an interest in the social sciences and the native abilities that we associate with the good language teacher never enter the profession simply because of the lack of social-science-based graduate language programs (see Jorden, 1982, for an excellent discussion of the problem). In many cases they are probably siphoned off into other professions such as translation or technical editing or international business. If they end up teaching at all, they probably take jobs in commercial language schools or they move into ESOL programs. ESOL, where the emphasis falls on practical results and measurable achievement, has long since broadened its base to include English for Specific Purposes (ESP) and othern non-literary approaches to language learning (Coffey, 1985; McDonough, 1984). The commonly-taught European languages lag far behind (Iodice, 1983; but see, for example, Bénouis, 1986, Hoegl, 1986).

Recently, however, we have seen numbers of successful efforts to link foreign languages and international studies, or foreign languages and the social sciences. Earlham College was an early entry into the field, in a program linking languages and the social sciences through the exchange of professors and team teaching; and the Pennsylvania Council on International Education recently organized a summer project involving a consortium of institutions in curricular planning and implementation (Burnett and Robinson, 1985). In 1981 an entire volume of the Northeast Conference *Reports* was devoted to this subject (Geno, 1981), as was the February 1985 issue of *Social Education* (see Bragaw and Loew, 1985), whose topic "Enriching Social Studies Through Language Studies" is likely to interest the college teacher as well as the secondary school teacher. (See also Gaudiani, 1983).

Forging links with colleagues in the social sciences requires a measure of diplomacy. Although many Ph.D. programs in the social sciences do require that their students demonstrate some competency in foreign languages, many social scientists have little or no command of foreign languages and have little occasion, by choice or by necessity, to use them in their work. They may be unconvinced of the importance of foreign languages in the curriculum or disturbed that members of foreign language departments are displaying an interest in "their" disciplines. Those social scientists directly involved in international work are, understandably, more likely to take a different view. However, just as an interest in the social sciences may be regarded as slightly odd among language teachers, so an active interest in international affairs may peg the social scientist on the periphery of his or her discipline, given the vagaries and professional self-images of the disciplines themselves.

There are many ways in which collaboration can be established in an academic community. The teacher of Spanish, for example, might identify the Latin Americanists on the faculty and those with an interest in Spanish history. Perhaps the office of international education or the dean can help by providing information on speakers of Spanish and people who have lived or studied in Spanish-speaking countries. Possibly some of these individuals might be included in the exchange of publications that the teacher has already established in the department. They might be invited in to participate in a Spanish class as informants on some aspect of Spanish or Latin American life. Language students could be encouraged to take their courses. In return, the Spanish teacher might offer to visit the social scientist's course or to assist students interested in using Spanish-language materials in the writing of term papers. Both parties could assist in the joint preparation of reading lists for their courses. Possibly they could even teach a course together, or offer a pair of linked courses that could simultaneously provide social science training and advanced language work. There are examples of linkages of this kind in numbers of institutions, and a few have established ongoing cooperation between the departments of social sciences and foreign languages.

Successful alliances may involve only two people or they may involve groups of people. Where interest is broad enough, it is possible to establish a faculty seminar or discussion group, meeting regularly to discuss curricular questions or to explore topics of common interest relating to the language communities in question. Possibly some modest funding might be obtained from the administration for materials or for visiting speakers. The cooperation might lead the group to invite a foreign scholar through the Fulbright program to assist in the development of cooperative groups and eventually in the establishment of programs of study abroad, special study trips, and possibly entire programs in area studies or international studies.

The cooperative effort that we have described here is based on a common interest in a particular language. Equally productive, however, and perhaps a little less obvious, is the formation of a group concerned with global studies, in which the language teacher takes on the role of informant for a particular language or part of the world. Major world events or trends are not seen in the same light in all parts of the world, as we know all too well. Hence, for example, reporting on Iran by the Paris-based *Le Monde* in the period before the revolution in that country was different from that by the leading United States newspapers; the French and Germans had quite different views on the April 1986 bombing of Libya from those current in the United States. In the same way, issues such as European security, or African famine, or the problem of acid rain, or foreign debt, or arms sales (and the facts and figures that go along with these phenomena) are presented differently in the European press. Some of the best reporting on Africa appears in French, and some of the most interesting stories on Latin America are carried in German periodicals. Needless to say, United States policy in Latin America is likely to be read quite differently in Caracas or Buenos Aires or even Santiago from the way it is read in Washington or New York.

Obtaining up-to-date materials in foreign languages may present some problems. We shall deal later with library cooperation. At this point we need only remind our readers that subscriptions to foreign language periodicals are not necessarily prohibitively expensive. Additional materials can be obtained from embassies and United Nations missions, or directly from government information services in the home countries.

We cannot stress too strongly the importance of making linkages with faculty members concerned with the interpretation of foreign and global affairs, either through formal faculty seminars or through informal discussion groups — or indeed through individual contacts. The linkage is important not only because it helps to broaden the knowledge and awareness of the language teacher but also because it brings to the social science classroom firsthand experience and materials from abroad. Frequently, courses in international politics and economics, or in global issues, rely heavily or even exclusively on English-language sources; and they almost never make use of foreign language press reports published as the course is occurring. What better way to establish the importance of language study in the minds of the students and to win the support of colleagues in the social sciences? As more colleges and universities move towards the institution of general education requirements — and the reinstitution of language requirements — the possibilities for cooperation multiply.

Such possibilities are not, of course, limited to the social sciences. Indeed, they are limited only by the imagination, ingenuity, and diplomacy of the language professor and colleagues. Cooperation might take place with philosophers, or natural scientists (especially those concerned with public policy), or with colleagues in the English department (König and Robbins, 1984). In all cases, the aim is essentially the same: to enrich the classroom in these other disciplines, to broaden one's own knowledge, and to persuade students and faculty members of the applicability of language study.

Cooperating with the Administration

Given its specific configuration of disciplines and programs, geographical location, and history, a college or university has a will of its own and a political structure that can be analyzed only by reference to numerous intangibles, not the least of which are the personalities of the individuals concerned. The foreign language professor anxious to create a climate favorable to language study on the campus must be sensitive to local eccentricities and power structures. In the first instance, of course, the professor must create good relationships with other members of the department and, if at all possible, should cooperate with departmental colleagues to raise the visibility of the department on the campus and make it an effective teaching unit as well as a local presence.

Much has been written on the management of departments of language and literature, and much progress has been made on strengthening them and increasing their responsiveness. Gaudiani's work in this area is particularly well known (Gaudiani and Herron, 1984), and the pages of the *ADFL Bulletin* often carry helpful articles (note, for example, its checklist for self-study). We shall not repeat here what has been said there, but will concentrate on the role of the *individual* in his or her relationship with the academic hierarchy. Much of what we suggest will apply equally well to departments.

We can identify in and around the campus a number of constituent groups and individuals who require particular attention and towards whom we should in effect develop a constant "policy" (Tonkin and Edwards, 1981, pp. 144–178). These groups, in addition to our colleagues on the faculty, and faculty governance structures, include: deans, vice-presidents, the president, those involved in student affairs and residences, the students themselves, alumni, trustees, and parents. The reader may be able to add further groups to the list, on the basis of local experience.

WORKING WITH THE HIERARCHY: VERTICAL COMMUNICATION

It is important to know one's senior administrators and to understand their backgrounds. It is equally important to understand the kinds of pressures under which they lead their lives and the principles on which they make their decisions (even deans and presidents have principles, tattered though those principles may sometimes appear to be). While we like to think that colleges and universities are intellectual havens where decisions are made on intellectual grounds, and while we are all too easily convinced that in the hands of administrators they are nothing more than devices for the pursuit of the almighty dollar, both of these views are useful only as rhetorical gambits and the truth lies somewhere between. Most colleges and universities are today engaged in efforts at self-preservation, and most actions by senior administrators can be explained in these terms. It is a process of constant compromise between budgetary pressures on the one hand, along with effective marketing strategies and efforts to broaden the clientele for higher education, and the preservation of the integrity of the institution on the other. Needless to say, this is not always a dichotomy, a collision of contrary forces. In many instances, the integrity of the institution may go hand in hand with good marketing or with sound budgetary practices. To the extent that the foreign language teacher can help the administrator to perceive a link between sound management and the allocation of resources to foreign languages, the foreign language departments are likely to prosper. Such groups as students, alumni, and parents (along with external groups like school superintendents or the public at large) may prove useful allies in this process. It is equally important to counter negative views where they arise.

Many administrators may well have some foreign experience. This experience may have involved study or work abroad, or foreign travel, or military service overseas. Some may have experience of foreign languages, indeed may speak or use them with a reasonable degree of fluency. Wherever such experience exists, we should build on it. If we detect in an administrator a particular interest in foreign affairs, or if we are aware of an interest in education in other countries, we should keep that individual informed. A copy of an interesting newspaper article or a note about some interesting new development is enough to maintain the contact. Most college and university administrators' time is extremely limited and they will only be embarrassed by too much material or too much detail. As an administrator who likes to keep in touch with developments in other countries, I am always pleased to receive notes or newspaper clippings (with brief summaries) from faculty members who indicate thereby that they do not regard me only as someone to whom they complain about merit increases or about the fact that their office door has not been repaired but that they also see in me someone who may be interested in the things that interest them. If nothing else, it means that we have something else to talk about than salaries or doors or the weather when we next meet at a faculty cocktail party.

In this regard faculty members should not feel abashed about telling their senior administration about what they do. If a professor goes to a conference to give a paper, or has an article accepted, or signs a contract for a book, a note to the dean, or the academic vice-president, or even the president may help to demonstrate that faculty members in foreign languages are involved and alive. If a visitor comes to the campus from a foreign country, perhaps a brief visit to the president or vice-president could be arranged, and if the foreign language professor is going abroad, perhaps a message of greeting from the president of his or her home institution can be directed to the president of the institution the professor is visiting. Such courtesies may seem obvious, but they are frequently neglected.

Deans have the most direct control over resource allocation and hence are particularly important members of the hierarchy. The effective department chair will cultivate a close relationship with the dean, characterized as much as possible by cooperation, tempered of course by firmness. The chair should be able to demonstrate that the members of the department are productive members of the institution, dedicated and involved teachers, willing participants in governance, and active in the scholarly and educational community. The case is strengthened if there is evidence that the department is interested in curricular experiment and change — something that perhaps comes more easily to the foreign language department, given the nature of the subject matter that it teaches and the need for a variety of delivery systems for the constituencies it serves. If it is also evident that the department is working closely with other departments, so much the better. The chair should also be able to demonstrate that the department is constantly seeking resources to support and finance its activities, through the writing of grant proposals, either on its own or in cooperation with other departments or such outside agencies as the public schools, or through the acquisition of outside funding for sabbaticals from such international programs as the Fulbright fellowships, the Guggenheim, ACLS or NEH fellowship programs. Curricular innovation should not, of course, be confined exclusively to the discovery of new ways to work with the existing audience, that is to say new ways of convincing students who would otherwise take sociology to take Spanish instead. While such efforts are commendable to the extent that they improve the overall quality of instruction, they do little to address budgetary issues and may even prove to be a drain on institutional resources. Equally important, or in some institutions more important, are ways of reaching new audiences and drawing new constituencies into the orbit of the institution.

The dean, in turn, must report to the vice-president. To what extent are foreign languages contributing to the cohesion of undergraduate programs? How central are languages to the general mission of the school? How effectively are they taught? How popular are they? How visible is the foreign language faculty on the campus and beyond? Again, if we can provide the dean with good arguments and demonstrable successes, the dean's bid for resources is made easier; and more resources, in turn, flow to foreign languages. The effort is made easier if there are other lines of communication between department and vice-president and if the vice-president is made a part of the life of the department by invitations to special events and a reasonable flow of information about activities in foreign languages.

One of the largest problems faced by any foreign language department in its dealings with deans and vice-presidents, and frequently with fellow faculty members as well, is the problem of inflated expectations. Foreign language teachers know how difficult it is to bring students to a working knowledge of a language. Brief exposure to that language, particularly in one-hour segments three times a week, may not be enough. However, colleagues often assume that languages well taught are easily learned, and they are perplexed that students who complete elementary language courses are often unable to put the language to practical use. A related assumption is that imposition of a language requirement as part of a general education program will automatically produce language competence among the students or that a shift to a proficiency-based program will turn a moribund requirement into an effective one at little or no extra cost. As long as language teaching is delivered in standard segments in large classes, the failure rate is bound to be high; and if the sheer organizational problems involved in running proficiency-based programs are not addressed, they too will fail to produce the desired results.

It is only fair to point out that language teachers, for their part, frequently use the difficulty of language learning as an excuse for poor results; or they avoid subjecting themselves to scrutiny by non-language faculty members or administrators out of a fear of unfavorable exposure. Administrators are often right in their expression of frustration at language departments that seem determined to resist change, but they also often fail to appreciate both the difficulty of language teaching and the intense level of engagement required of the effective teacher.

This suggests, then, that some intelligent communication is required between foreign language faculty members and their administrators. The faculty members must show the administrators that they are current with their field and that their teaching applies the best methods available. They must be able to talk knowledgeably about methodology and about new developments in the field. At the same time, they must work to educate their deans and vice-presidents about language and language learning. For their part, the administrators will continue to raise questions; continue to ask for better results. They should be treated rationally, politely, and diplomatically. Nothing riles administrators more than being told that they do not know what they are talking about (a frailty hardly confined to administrators).

If it behooves us to draw upon, and build upon, the international experience of administrators, it is still more important to turn those with little or no international experience into internationalists. Here, too, the key to success is contact and communication. Values in the academy being what they are, there are few administrators who would not wish to be considered cosmopolitan and aware of the wider world. Hence there exists in most people a predisposition to become involved in international activities. Opportunities abound. They range from such simple matters as putting administrators together with foreign students or students returning from study abroad to organizing visits for administrators to study programs overseas or involving them in international missions of the college or university.

THE PRESIDENT

The level of involvement of a president in the day to day operations of the campus varies enormously from campus to campus and is in part a function of individual style. Particularly on smaller campuses, much of what is important in the cultivation of relationships with other officials holds true for presidents as well. Some presidents, despite their external responsibilities, stay close to the faculty and to academic programs. In numerous instances, the ultimate decisions on academic priorities are made by management teams that include the president or by the president in concert with the chief academic officer. Hence, keeping the president informed and sympathetic is extremely important.

Presidents' time is always limited. Most presidents are constantly engaged in a battle to increase their productivity, reduce the pressures to which they are subjected, and delegate the responsibilities that they feel able to pass on to others. At the same time, they are able to exercise a good deal of choice as to how they spend their time. Some stay on the campus working with internal campus groups, while their deans and vice-presidents do much of the travelling. Others are constantly on the road, visiting alumni, raising funds, or representing the institution at the regional or national level. Regardless of how their time is spent, they are constantly interacting with others; and the opinions that they express and the information that they share are closely noted and carefully heeded. They serve as advocates for the institution in much of what they do, and they like to know what the achievements and the problems of their constituents are. They can, of course, serve as advocates for particular educational priorities, particularly in their dealings with legislators, national organizations, funding agencies, and donors. Many presidents have some measure of international experience. Some travel abroad quite frequently on behalf of their institutions or as members of academic delegations. Obviously they should be encouraged in such activities, however skeptical we may be about the actual degree of grassroots contact that they have while they are abroad or however they may occasionally be faulted for believing all that they are told.

If the individual faculty member has contacts abroad, he or she may wish to use them to increase a president's experience in the international arena. An invitation to visit a foreign institution or to see a study program abroad may be enough to convince a president to take a trip overseas or to include this visit in the itinerary. While occasionally such excursions may not have the desired effect, in general the more international exposure a president has, the greater the level of his or her commitment.

Keeping a president informed of developments in foreign languages on the campus requires careful orchestration. Communications on such matters should be short, simple, and easy to remember. While it may be a good idea to send full documentation on a new program or a special activity to a president, a brief covering note summarizing its contents should always be appended, so that the president does not have to read the entire document to obtain the salient facts. Particularly in large institutions, it may be advisable to keep the president's assistants apprised of such matters, so that they too can serve as advocates and allies. No one is more important in this regard than the assistant for legislative relations, where such an official exists. In the present political environment, legislation having a bearing on foreign language education and international affairs is constantly on the agenda of the United States Congress and of many state legislatures. Often one's local congressman or state legislator may wield considerable influence in shaping or approving such legislation. Harried college officials may be more than willing to accept a faculty member's assistance in formulating a position on particular items of legislation, and the president may well be able to raise with legislators particular pieces of legislation or to advocate particular action. The progress of federal foreign language legislation is relatively easily followed in such publications as the *Public Awareness Newsletter* of ACTFL, the circulars of JNCL/CLOIS, or the *Chronicle of Higher Education*, and in institutions with legislative affairs officers that individual may be able to assist in securing up-to-date information or intervening with legislative aides. Presidents are bombarded with legislative alerts from the major national organizations, such as the American Council on Education and NASULGC, and most probably go unheeded; but a careful effort by the foreign language department to follow legislation and to intervene at the right moment can help legislative efforts considerably. Presidents also communicate with their fellows in other institutions, and hence the well-informed president can serve as indirect advocate with other campuses as well. It may also prove profitable to encourage presidents to form pressure groups with their counterparts at other institutions on particular legislative efforts. Understandably, they are particularly sensitive to legislation offering financial opportunities or providing direct benefits to their own institutions; and it is advisable to appeal to such self-interest where arguments can be found.

Presidents speak to school boards, they talk to parents, they are invited by local organizations to address them on burning issues of the day. The president who knows little about foreign languages or does not care about international education can do incalculable harm to the cause of foreign languages. No president should be ignored, however competent or incompetent he or she may appear to be and no matter how little he or she seems interested in languages. The question is not *whether* to keep the president informed, but *how* to do it. Where formal speeches are involved, different presidents follow different paths. For my own part, I rely heavily on notes prepared by members of my staff; but if I deliver a prepared text I generally write it myself. Some presidents always handle their own speeches, and others rely on writers. Where assistants and speech writers are involved, they need as much, or more, information as the president needs.

On the campus, the president may prove something of an unguided missile. It is important that in informal conversations with students the president reinforce the message that we wish to convey, and that the same occur in contacts with the faculty. Again, the key to success in these areas is good communication. However, we should also recognize that the influence of the president on the campus is limited. Some years ago, in a book on internationalizing the campus (Tonkin and Edwards, 1981) my co-author and I stressed that grassroots efforts are doomed to failure without leadership from the top, and that the co-opting of the leadership (not to put too fine a point on it) was essential to success. It is evident from the foregoing that my views have not changed. Now, however, as a college president I am more than ever convinced that leadership from the top without grassroots support is equally doomed to failure. In short, cooperation between grassroots and treetops (to say nothing of the links between the two) is the best guarantee of success.

LATERAL CONTACTS

There are, of course, many people on the campus whose international agendas are similar to those of the foreign language faculty and with whom it is possible to cooperate in approaches to members of the administration. Here, too, the value of collaboration with colleagues in other departments will be evident. It is particularly important to work closely with the campus office of international education or, where the various functions of study abroad, foreign students, international curriculum development, development work, and the maintenance of interinstitutional contacts are not handled through a single office, with the various offices concerned. In general, international activities are strengthened when such an office exists as a single unit and foreign language faculty members may wish to work to bring such consolidation about if the responsibilities are divided among several offices. Foreign language faculty members may be able to assist the international office in contacts with foreign students, both before and after admission. They may be able to provide advice on study abroad, both in their own geographical area and elsewhere. Their advice and assistance may be valuable in the planning and execution of exchange agreements with foreign universities or of development projects in Third World countries. Indeed, foreign language professors may be able to show institutions with little international experience how projects of these kinds can be developed. There is no institution so small or so parochial that international contacts have no place in its programs.

Much of what has already been said about deans and vice-presidents holds for the other offices on campus. A good working relationship with officials responsible for student affairs and for residences can lead to greater attention to international programming on campus. Where funds are available for bringing visiting speakers to campus or scheduling cultural activities, perhaps some of those funds can be used to bring in speakers from abroad or visitors with particular expertise in international affairs, especially foreign languages — or performers from other countries on tour in the United States. An increasing number of institutions run special residential programs, such as language houses or floors, or living-learning programs with particular thematic emphases. Projects of this kind can be set up in the international area through cooperation with residence staff.

The list of people whose help may be secured to advance foreign languages on the campus is as long as the list of officials in the campus telephone book. Generally such help will be forthcoming when the foreign language professor can offer help in return. Perhaps the admissions office needs assistance in the recruitment of foreign students, or perhaps it can be persuaded to do more in this area with the cooperation of faculty members familiar with other countries and the challenges of communication across cultures. Perhaps the athletics department can be encouraged to arrange tours abroad or to play visiting teams from abroad. One of the most successful international activities at my own institution was a trip to France by our basketball team. Not only was **it the first trip** abroad for several of the players, but also for several coaches and faculty **members as** well. In short, it reached a group of individuals relatively unfamiliar with **foreign** countries, reducing their fear of things foreign as well as augmenting enroll-**ments in Frenc**h in the following year.

Above all, it is important to work with the campus office in charge of public information. International activities make good press, and such offices are generally on the lookout for material for press releases. On some campuses it may be advisable to prepare a draft of a proposed press release so that it is easy for the office to put it out. In other cases, the office may supply a writer, or may assign someone to report on international developments regularly. Such a person should then become an object of cultivation by the canny foreign language department. All manner of subjects are good for press releases. If a group of students is travelling abroad, the public information office may be interested in doing hometown releases on each of them. If a foreign language faculty member wins an award or participates in a conference or develops a new program, such events may make good stories for the local press. Developments in particular parts of the world, or points of view gleaned from reading the foreign press, may provide the faculty member with an opportunity to write a feature story or op-ed piece that the public information office can then place in the press. Equally important is on-campus publicity; and particular efforts should be made to use in-house newsletters for stories on foreign language developments, including, of course, the student newspaper.

Finally, a general observation about cooperation on the campus: people like to feel a sense of ownership; they like to have a stake in whatever initiative they take. Wily administrators say that they always try to make the faculty think that the faculty thought of an idea first, and the wise faculty member with a good idea will always try to persuade the department chair or the dean to come up with the idea as though out of the blue. Academic programs, indeed all campus programs, whose ownership is shared, are most likely to succeed, and certainly most likely to persist.

Students, Parents, and Beyond

STUDENTS

Whole books are written on academic administration and organization with barely a mention of students. Even in today's climate of enrollment management and institutional marketing, it is surprising how seldom we stop to ask what students want and why they want it. Not all that they want is bad, nor are their motives invariably base. They are, however, seriously underinformed about the world; and there is some evidence that their knowledge of other countries is actually declining. Given the increasing role that foreign affairs will play in the domestic affairs of the United States in the years ahead, it becomes essential that we do all that we can to raise their consciousness of global affairs and their understanding of cultural diversity.

Our most immediate contact with the students is in the classroom. Attitudes displayed in the classroom and opinions expressed may stay with the students long after they leave our hands. The foreign language professor is particularly well placed to assist the students in coming to an understanding of the larger world and to convey to them the value of language study as a way of expanding their horizons. It is helpful if their study of languages has a demonstrable relationship with the other things that they do and if they can put the language learned to practical use. Such considerations should enter into curriculum planning and the preparation of syllabi, and they should also cause us to think about how students' language competence can be maintained after they leave the language course. One way, to which we have already alluded, is by encouraging them to use their knowledge of the foreign language in courses in other disciplines. Departments might also explore the establishment of language clubs, in which former students are welcome and whose programs are geared to students with relatively limited language competence. Such clubs also serve as devices for drawing in faculty members from other fields, making links with foreign students, and encouraging cooperation at all levels. Club programs could include some public relations activities, such as celebration of Foreign Language Week or national independence days. They may also serve as fora for visiting speakers. Student activities fees may well be available to provide funding.

The problem facing the language teacher, and lying behind much of my argument here, is the problem of bringing the student to an adequate level of competence to put the language to practical use. In this connection, there is no substitute for foreign study and travel. All students—language majors and non-language majors alike—should be encouraged to study abroad. It is not necessary for one's own college to offer a particular program in a particular country: there are hundreds of programs, of varying quality and sophistication, offered by dozens of United States colleges and available to the average student. All that is needed is to locate them and, if possible, do some personal checking on their quality. Foreign study is not prohibitively expensive. For the non-language major, numerous programs of foreign study offer curricula that go beyond the culture and language of the country in question and provide opportunities for study of the social sciences or even in some cases the natural sciences. Particularly competent students who have spent time abroad may be willing to visit foreign language classes from time to time, assist with drills, or otherwise help with the course.

In our efforts to convince students of the value of language study, the students themselves are our best advocates. They should be encouraged to raise the issue wherever they can. Articles in student newspapers, for example, or talks to student organizations can do much to raise the consciousness of the campus. Students can also assist in the running of residential programs, in work with foreign student admissions, or in helping foreign students adjust to life in this country. Their assistance should be used in informational meetings on language study organized by the department. Here, too, they can often be more convincing with fellow students than we can.

Our primary goal must, of course, be to attract the student through the department door and retain that student in our classes. This means, as we all recognize, that these introductory courses must be well taught and consistently interesting. Not only should our best teachers be responsible for introductory courses, working, where convenient, with teaching assistants (who should not be let loose on new students without adequate supervision); but also we should analyze very carefully the nature of our clientele. The mere fact that a student has had a year or two of high school language does not necessarily mean that that student fully understands the relativity of language or the techniques for learning languages. Adequate attention to such matters in the early weeks of the semester may avoid problems later on. Exercises teaching a student how to discover the salient features of a language, perhaps by comparing several languages, may be more valuable than a few weeks of standard Spanish or French. One language teacher of my acquaintance occasionally uses Romanian as a kind of linguistic propedeutic model; several use Esperanto (Szerdahelyi, 1966).

We can help build our enrollment by seeking non-traditional students and by creating special offerings for special groups, including teachers anxious to augment language knowledge or to become certified as language teachers, business people requiring intensive training, and even alumni wishing to renew or maintain language study begun years earlier in our own departments.

PARENTS

There is a great deal of support for language study among the parents of our students. A public survey conducted some years ago by the University of Michigan revealed that no less than 50 percent of those polled wished that they could speak another language and 84 percent of parents with children under 16 encourage them to study foreign languages (Eddy, 1979). In short, most people support the *idea* of foreign language education. The opinions of parents continue to be an important factor in determining what students study, and hence keeping them informed about foreign language study on the campus and involving them in appropriate ways is important. Here are a few ideas.

- Many campuses publish newsletters for parents. We should make sure that they publish stories on foreign language programs from time to time.
- Some campuses have parents' organizations. Perhaps there are ways of addressing their board or keeping their board informed about new developments in foreign language programs.
- Parents of students in foreign languages may themselves have international experience or foreign language expertise. They might be invited to meet with department members to provide advice on curriculum or to attend and participate in classes.
- The department might organize a special program on Parents' Day, or set up a display in a location where parents can see it.
- Special efforts should be made to convince parents of the value of study abroad. Students almost invariably consult with their parents before making the decision, and frequently parents are reluctant to give their consent out of fear of the dangers involved or concern at the distance.

ALUMNI

All of these ideas, with the exception of the last, apply equally well to alumni. They, too, can be addressed through the pages of the alumni magazine. They, too, can be involved in the life of the department. A few departments try to maintain contact with former majors, either in cooperation with their institution's alumni office or quite separately. Some even produce their own newsletters directed primarily at alumni. Such an effort, while it is time-consuming and requires systematic attention, can bear fruit in many ways. Alumni success stories serve as stimuli to current students; alumni in other countries may serve as useful contacts and as suppliers of classroom materials; when the time for Annual Giving comes round, the department may well find itself the recipient of restricted gifts for student aid or other purposes. Indeed, the involvement of the department in annual giving campaigns may be welcomed by the development office, especially if the department maintains good records on former students and can assist with specific information.

In cooperation with the alumni office, the department might consider offering a special summer study program abroad, combining tourism with lectures and reading. There are numerous models for such programs and many institutions offer them. If the institution has an alumni college, perhaps the department can offer a special program to update the language skills of alumni.

TRUSTEES

The trustees' influence in the internal affairs of a college or university, and their visibility on campus, varies considerably from institution to institution (Tonkin and Edwards, 1981, pp. 161–163). In some institutions the trustees are a shadowy group, meeting behind closed doors on their infrequent visits to campus or holding their meetings in an entirely different city. In other cases they are frequent visitors to the campus, either together or singly, and are relatively easy to approach. Most trustees, even if they are involved in campus life, are conscious of the fact that the running of the institution is in the hands of the president; and they will tend to avoid taking initiatives without the president's knowledge and tacit approval. There may also be a general awareness on the campus that faculty approaches to the trustees should be cleared through the president's office.

A normal feature of board meetings at many institutions is a briefing on academic programs or other aspects of campus life. Topics are often chosen for their intrinsic interest or because they are of topical interest. Perhaps the suggestion can be planted with the administration that a briefing on foreign language programs would be a good idea, especially when there are new directions or initiatives to be reported. Such a briefing offers an ideal opportunity to establish contact with the trustees as a group and to legitimize ongoing contacts with individual board members. Trustees are normally highly influential citizens with numerous public contacts. Like the president, they can serve as strong advocates for foreign language study or, if they are neglected, they can have great negative influence. If good personal contacts with individual trustees can be established, they should be kept informed, much as the senior administration is kept informed, of new developments. Trustees with knowledge of foreign languages might be brought into the orbit of the department through invitations to special events. Particular attention might be given to those trustees with political contacts or with other contacts in education.

The Campus Environment: The Role of the Administration

THE ISSUES

Although there are limits to the extent to which administrators can influence the details of the curriculum, they are the largest single influence on working conditions, including the physical surroundings in which learning takes place. While colleagues can make the average faculty member's work pleasant or unpleasant, easier or relatively more difficult, the administration controls the reward system. For this reason, if for no other, it is important that senior administrators know and understand the circumstances in which foreign language faculty members go about their business.

Broadly defined, there are six aspects of the environment of language teaching that require the active attention of the administration. Faculty members should do their best to work with the administration to establish guidelines and programs in these six areas.

- Appointment, reappointment, and tenure. What types of contributions are expected of the language teacher and how will quality be assessed and rewarded?
- Resources. What library support is provided? What technological resources are available? Is there funding to purchase classroom materials or for other activities?
- Modes of delivery. To what extent is the teacher confined to standard methods of classroom teaching, in standard blocks of time easily handled by the course scheduling computer?
- Methods and approaches. To what extent are teachers encouraged to try new approaches, and is there time available to learn new approaches and develop new materials?
- Physical setting. Does the administration encourage international activities on campus? Are students accustomed to an international atmosphere on campus?
- Burnout and reinvigoration. Constant language teaching, at the same level and with the same daily frustrations, leads to early burnout. Does the administration provide opportunities for teachers to return from time to time to the country of the language they teach?

APPOINTMENTS, REAPPOINTMENTS, AND TENURE

It is essential that the administration spell out with reasonable clarity its expectations of language teachers, especially with respect to tenure. Since the acquisition of language is essentially the acquisition of a skill, language differs from other fields, and teachers can often do relatively little to advance their own scholarship through teaching. If scholarship is important, what kind of scholarship should they pursue? Is literary scholarship the only kind ultimately acceptable, or will work on linguistics, or applied linguistics, or teaching methodology, be taken equally seriously? Indeed, what is the relationship between teaching and research? The answers to these questions will vary from institution to institution and there are no universally right answers, but they should be spelled out to some extent. Each language teacher should try to work with the department chair to develop some general principles, applicable to individual cases, or, preferably, applicable to the department as a whole. The administration must be convinced that it is in the interest of all to have a statement of common standards that go beyond official institution-wide statements about tenure.

RESOURCES

The question of library resources is particularly complex. In most fields, it is relatively easy to keep the library supplied with a list of departmental needs. Funding may be lacking to buy everything that is requested, but priorities are relatively easy to determine. With foreign languages the case is altered, since the linguistic medium of a given acquisition may be as important as its contents. One of the first tasks confronting a foreign language department, and one that many have not in fact performed, is to discover what books and periodicals in a given language the library actually holds. Since books are not ordinarily organized by language, this may be quite difficult to establish. Perhaps a cooperative effort can be worked out with the library for a rough inventory of, say, resources in Spanish, including Spanish-language works in all fields. This inventory can be made available to Spanish teachers (and perhaps faculty members in other fields) and kept on file at the reference desk. Expanding the collection will require the assistance of faculty members. In some instances, it may be possible to purchase foreign language books through the library allocations to other departments. At the same time, purchasing foreign language materials can be expensive, and the department may run into some resistance from librarians unfamiliar with working with materials in languages other than English and reluctant to handle the problems of cataloguing. Depending on the size of the institution and the nature of the collection, foreign language professors may be able to work through their own contacts to obtain foreign language publications for the library less expensively, and they may be able to assist library professionals with cataloguing. Particular attention should also be given to the acquisition of some periodicals, particularly general-interest magazines and newspapers. Sometimes these latter materials should be purchased directly by the departments, so that they are readily available in the department office and can be used in teaching.

Potentially, language departments are heavy users of technology, and hence maintaining close relationships with those in charge of audiovisual facilities, educational technology, and computers is essential. Again, it is important that the administration take into consideration the needs of language departments, which may also extend to the acquisition of satellite dishes, videodiscs, taped materials, and the like. But it is also important that departments submit reasoned and carefully documented requests based on research, direct user experience, consultation with other users, and "comparison shopping." This is particularly necessary because of the high cost and rapid obsolescence of such equipment. In short, some systematic effort should be made on all campuses to examine the support needs of the foreign language faculty and to build budgets accordingly—while taking into consideration the numerous ways in which self-help and cooperation can solve many problems.

MODES OF DELIVERY

In our list of essential conditions we mentioned modes of delivery primarily because this most important of questions is often ignored. The person in charge of course scheduling is unlikely to be sympathetic to language departments asking for odd schedules or strange combinations of hours, nor is the average curriculum committee enthusiastic about making exceptions. Many language teachers, perhaps most, would surely agree, however, that the standard way of teaching languages, in the classroom setting, with 20 or 30 students, three or four times a week, is not the best or the only way. There is a limit to the extent to which we can convince our clients, the students, to sign up for more intensive programs, in longer or shorter blocks or in different settings; but it hardly helps to be told by an insensitive administrator that "the computer cannot accommodate" our needs or that time slots cannot be adjusted. An administration willing to assist with alternative modes can do much to help the language teacher, especially when this willingness extends to a readiness to recalculate work loads and to adjust expectations in full-time equivalents generated by the department.

METHODS AND APPROACHES

The issue of approaches to language teaching is closely related to the issue of flexibility in scheduling and the like, because some methods require special conditions. Today language teachers are experimenting with interactive videodisc, with linked computers and voice-synthesizers, and, at the other end of the technological scale, with telephone courses. The shift away from a pure audio-lingual approach has not been occasioned solely by advances in technology but also by changes in our assumptions about how learning takes place. There are those who attempt to establish empirically which methods work and which do not, but building good experimental models in this field is notoriously difficult, since such variables as teacher enthusiasm and student motivation tend to undermine reasonable comparison. However, the current state of foreign language teaching is characterized by bewildering eclecticism as Suggestopedia vies with Rassias, Total Physical Response with the Silent Way, and so on. In a global sense, however, it is clear that people learn languages when they have to and that, regardless of method, those who know that they must survive in a given language environment tend to learn faster than those for whom learning a language is nothing more than an academic requirement. In short, there is no perfect way of teaching languages (Higgs, 1984).

The issue is complicated by recent emphasis on proficiency, and particularly oral proficiency (Byrnes and Canale, 1987; Higgs, 1984; Omaggio, 1985). While there are some who question our new-found enthusiasm for proficiency-based language requirements and competency-based instruction, the proficiency-based movement has brought about a remarkably strong alliance between administrators, who are looking for accountability and results, and language teachers—an alliance which has led to increases in language enrollments and new curricular emphasis on foreign languages all across the country. We should, of course, be wary of inflated expectations; the mere establishment of a proficiency-based requirement will not automatically make students competent. First, we must assume that language teachers, faced with the requirement that their students become proficient, will improve their teaching. (If nothing happens in this regard, why make the change?) Second, we must assume that the threat of failure

and the prospect of measurable success will motivate students to learn. Third, we must assume that the faculty is actually capable of measuring proficiency. If all of the above conditions are fulfilled, we will presumably still find ourselves with student failures on our hands. Have provisions been made for remedial work for these students? Will the labor-intensive teaching required to bring them to acceptable levels be taken into adequate consideration by administrators concerned about productivity? Furthermore, will the sheer difficulty of handling large numbers of oral proficiency tests, and the amount of time it takes to administer and evaluate them be recognized by these same administrators?

The average language department appears to be faced, almost on an ongoing basis, with a major retooling problem. With so many new approaches to language teaching circulating in the language teaching community, it is obviously undesirable that every language teacher or every department respond to them all, turning everything upside down every other year and destroying continuity. It is, however, essential that language teachers be given ample opportunity, in the form of released time and scholarly leaves, to explore the new approaches, to update their knowledge of the linguistics on which new methods are based, and to prepare new materials. A generous policy on faculty development, including travel money for conferences and workshops, is the single most important contribution the administration can make to the effective teaching of languages. It is particularly important in departments that are heavily tenured and require motivation for change.

In short, the emphasis on oral proficiency, the wholesale reintroduction or strengthening of language requirements at the college level and of language instruction not only in high schools but also in elementary schools, coupled with a new-found enthusiasm for language among those responsible for educational policy from the federal level on down — these threaten to turn our euphoria into disillusionment as, once again, expectations run ahead of results.

The oral proficiency movement is as much a political movement as an educational movement. For many foreign language teachers, the ACTFL guidelines have become a bible. Workshops and training sessions for every phase of proficiency (how to implement it, provide for it, make it work) are routine to every conference and their results appear in every professional journal. Has the language teaching community, trapped by falling enrollments, public indifference, and the global spread of English, made a promise it cannot keep, and contributed to a rhetorical pattern that feeds false expectations? As an administrator, I welcome this sense of responsibility on the part of foreign language teachers and the sudden surge in public interest in languages that accompanies it, but I try to remain conscious of the fact that success will not come as easily or as cheaply as some of us imagine. Indeed I occasionally wonder whether the very quantity of suffering experienced by many of our present politicians and educators and business people years ago in the language classroom does not somehow reinforce their desire to impose language learning on the young.

SETTING

Responsiveness to the special needs of language teachers on the part of the administration may go hand in hand with a general openness to international programming and the creation of an international atmosphere on the campus. If colleges and universities are genuinely part of the world of learning, and if they are truly one of the social institutions that we use to gather knowledge about the larger world, they should

look and feel international. Internationalizing the campus involves not only programmatic change but also a kind of physical responsiveness, triggered, above all, by a willingness on the part of middle-level administrators to consider ways of strengthening the international dimension of what they do (see Tonkin and Edwards, 1981, pp. 180–203). The bookstore can perhaps increase its purchase of foreign books, convocation series can feature foreign speakers, foreign touring groups can be booked into on-campus performance series. Even such simple-minded matters as posting announcements of departmental activities in foreign languages or running foreign language advertisements in the student newspaper can help, in their small way, to raise student consciousness of foreign languages. For my own part, my ideal is that every student should encounter at least once a day a foreign language text that he or she would like to understand, in short that texts in foreign languages be a standard part of the campus environment.

BURNOUT AND REINVIGORATION

Finally, there is the matter of burnout. All faculty members, if they are obliged to teach the same courses year after year or deal with the same problems, risk burnout sooner or later. But for language teachers the problem is particularly acute. First, the teaching of elementary language courses, the staple of many language departments, requires repetition year after year of essentially the same material, regardless of changes in methodology or textbooks. Second, as we have already noted, the level of in-class engagement with the students is unusually high. Third, the foreign language teacher is, in effect, a citizen in exile: the language that he or she teaches is generally spoken in some other part of the world, remote from the teacher's daily life. Returning to that social environment from time to time is particularly necessary for most foreign language professors. For this reason, as much as any other, a generous leave policy, preferably with travel support, is important for healthy language teaching.

Most of the comments in this section have been directed primarily at administrators. In our discussion of libraries we have seen that much can be achieved through cooperation and self-help. The same is true in other matters too. Departments should be willing to cover for colleagues anxious to take leaves; language faculty members should do what they can, with or without the administration, to increase the international atmosphere on campus; departments should have information on methodological advances and should use faculty travel as a device for gathering information for the common good. Ideally, self-help will be supplemented with administrative cooperation, for the benefit of language programs generally.

External Constituencies: The Schools and the Public

The nation faces a crisis in the preparation of teachers of foreign languages for elementary and secondary schools. In several states recent mandates requiring high school language study or expanding language teaching into the elementary schools have created a severe teacher shortage. At the same time, many of the old problems faced by our public schools, particularly the problem of articulation, or linkage between the offerings at one level and those at another, remain. In recent years, spurred by such programs as Academic Alliances, the common interests of public school and college teachers have become increasingly apparent. Others will deal with linkage between public schools and colleges elsewhere in this volume. No constituency beyond the campus

is more important than the public schools, and cooperation in faculty development, curriculum building and coordination of resources is essential. The Academic Alliance model provides an excellent means of linkage, but the enterprising language professor need not wait for collective action. A language professor can act independently to create informal linkages. Public school teachers have much to tell the college teacher about what works in the classroom and what does not, and much to tell prospective teachers about conditions in elementary and secondary schools. They can prove valuable classroom resources and, just as the professor can share resources and ideas with departmental colleagues, so that cooperation can be extended to the public schools. Language professors can assist their colleagues in the public schools by speaking up for foreign languages in school board hearings and by seeking to reach board members with their concerns.

Beyond the schools is the larger public, dauntingly diverse but crucially important to the success of foreign language programs. The language professor is well placed to influence that larger public. We have already discussed some indirect routes to the public by means of the president and the trustees. Here are a few additional ideas on more direct approaches.

- Business. Almost certainly your college or university has ties with the local chamber of commerce. Identify who is involved with this connection and suggest a talk to the chamber on language needs in business, or an informal discussion with a few business leaders. Suggest an article in the chamber's newsletter.
- The press. Work through your campus's public information office to reach the local press with articles and stories on languages and their importance. There is a wealth of material from language-related organizations to draw upon.
- Service clubs. Look for faculty members who are members of service clubs and propose yourself or your colleagues as possible speakers at future meetings.
- Television and radio. The campus public information office will probably be able to help here too. You can also make direct contact with stations to convince them to run public service announcements on special occasions such as Foreign Language Week.
- Libraries. Work with local libraries to strengthen and publicize foreign language holdings, and encourage your students and colleagues to use the materials.
- Proclamations. Foreign Language Week offers an ideal opportunity to convince your president to issue a proclamation (with the attendant news release and perhaps a photograph or two). The mayor's office can be approached with a similar goal in mind.

Good ideas on public relations are not hard to come by (see, for example, Royer and McKim, 1981; Galloway, 1981; Wallach, 1984). Indeed, the possibilities for such activities are limited only by the time and the ingenuity of the people involved. Those people could include some of your own students, perhaps in collaboration with a journalism class, or linked specifically with departmental activities.

Is the Academy Ready for Today's Language Study?

The situation of language and the model of language study that I have described differs significantly from our received notions on such matters. At the beginning of this essay I suggested that the language teaching community had made enormous strides over the past ten years in adapting to changing needs and that it had gained signifi-

cantly in political sophistication. But in my opinion it still has far to go if it is to answer the needs of the nation and overcome the accumulated misorientation of past years. The reality is that language study in our colleges and universities, despite all of the changes of recent years, remains badly out of touch with the world of language itself. The college and university environment is characterized particularly by the following:

- A split between the situation of the major European languages and that of the less commonly taught languages. The former are more closely associated with under-graduate education, literary study, and traditional methodology: the latter are associated with graduate education, area studies, and less traditional approaches, and also with government funding. The relationship between the two and their relative place in higher education remain uncertain and obscure. (See Lambert, 1984; Jorden, 1982.)

- A failure to engage the language needs of business and other special groups, includ-ing the military and the foreign service. Most language training for these groups takes place either through specially organized institutions, such as the Defense Language Institute and the Foreign Service Institute, or through commercial language schools. (On the scope of corporate education, see Eurich, 1985.)

- A failure to recognize the role of language in the larger world and to engage directly the implication of this role. Related to this issue is the need for language teachers to become involved in the formulation of national policy on language education. Much progress has been made, but more is necessary.

In this Report I have been concerned more with the situation of the "traditional" language professor, the teacher of French, Spanish, or German, than with those involved in area studies programs who teach the less commonly taught languages. If these tra-ditional language professors are to capture the language market and to expand the catchment area of the university, as it has been expanded in other fields, to embrace the older student and the student concerned with career advancement and practical skills, they must break out of their dependency on literary training and study. What is called for is nothing less than the complete revision of doctoral programs in language and literature to emphasize the use of language in all its facets and to give due atten-tion to linguistics, particularly in its applied aspects, to a much greater degree than at present. There must be room in the program for the social sciences, ideally a social sciences track leading to the doctorate. Attention must be given to language pedagogy, language for special purposes, educational technology. As for literature, it should be-come one element in a larger whole; and literature professors should be encouraged to forge links with comparative literature or to create general literature programs separ-ated from language doctorates. Keeping the study of literature strong is important for the future of the humanities, but it should not be confused with the teaching of lan-guages (Tonkin, 1985).[2]

The curriculum offered by a language department to its undergraduate students and to other student clienteles should reflect this diversity. The department should learn everything it can from the techniques of commercial language schools and from the teachers of English to Speakers of Other Languages. There should be an adequate array of social-science-based introductory language courses, as well as literature-based courses, and these courses should be designed to bring the student as rapidly as possible to the practical utilization of language skills. Immersion courses should be offered both for regular undergraduate and for outside groups. Special-purpose courses should be pro-vided for the business community and for older students anxious to acquire an applica-

ble skill (Eveslage, 1986). If the staff of the department is unsuitable for such tasks, resources should be expended and incentives provided to retrain faculty members and to hire new ones. At a time when the available pool of college-age students is shrinking in most areas of the United States, survival depends on the expansion of markets.

Emphasis must fall on the achievement of results. Students leaving the program must be competent in those aspects of language that the department undertook to teach them. They must be able to use their newly acquired skills in practical ways. Where possible, the department should provide programs designed to maintain already acquired skills and to revive atrophied language knowledge.

The so-called traditional languages are our largest language teaching resource, but it is not necessarily true that the greatest national need for foreign language skills lies in Europe. Chinese, Arabic, and Japanese compete for our attention and should perhaps receive greater priority in our schools and colleges. Personally, I am skeptical about our ability to provide a student who has no knowledge of foreign languages with a working knowledge of any of these languages in the time normally available. While I am certainly not opposed to including non-European languages in the undergraduate curriculum, I believe that we should work to make the European languages bridges to these more difficult undertakings, just as some language professors use Esperanto or Latin as an introduction to language study. We should seek to foster cooperation between teachers of European and non-European languages. This is also a practical way of building the European languages into a national language policy.

We are at present, willy-nilly, engaged in the formulation of such a policy, in which French, German, and Spanish could have a role, along with the strategically important languages, such as Russian, Arabic, Japanese, and Chinese, or from which the commonly taught languages could easily be excluded. United States Secretary of Education Bennett and others have recently sought to remind us of the importance of the humanities and of the role of language in general education (Bennett, 1984). They have placed heavy emphasis on our European roots and in effect advanced a conservative educational philosophy that is questionable in today's world. But the European languages are not only a window on Europe: they are also a window on the world. To the extent that we can link European languages with a new internationalism, a new attempt to chart a course for the United States on the international scene, teachers of the European languages can find a place for themselves in the nation's language policy by stressing simultaneously our culture's ties with Europe, the worldwide influence of European languages, and the use of European languages as a means of transition to the non-European. Their success in this and related endeavors will determine whether the academy is truly ready for today's language study.

Notes

1 The author wishes to acknowledge the assistance of Professor Maureen Regan in the preparation of this article.

2 On the problems of graduate education, the reader is particularly referred to a recent issue of the *ADFL Bulletin* (1986, *17*, [3]), devoted in part to "Graduate Education in Languages, Literatures, and the Humanities." This issue contains the "Resolutions and Recommendations of the National Conference on Graduate Education in the Foreign Language Fields" (November 1985), which include several of the innovations that I have also advocated in this essay. See also the article by Devens, which makes somewhat depressing reading, and the survey of graduate programs by Devens and Bennett. The latter indicates that, of the 112 pro-

grams surveyed, only two percent require coursework in a non-humanities field, and none of these is a program in the more commonly taught languages. Only 37 percent require coursework in methods or techniques of language teaching.

References

ADFL. A checklist for self-study for departments of languages and literatures. *ADFL Bulletin*, 1985, *16*, (3), 45–53.

Bennett, W. J. *To reclaim a legacy: A report on the humanities in higher education*. Washington, DC: National Endowment for the Humanities, 1984.

Bénouis, M. K. French for specific purposes: The Hawaiian experience. *Foreign Language Annals*, 1986, *19*, 13–17.

Bernstein, B. *Class, codes and control, vol. 1: Theoretical studies towards a sociology of language*. London: Routledge and Kegan Paul, 1971.

Bragaw, D. H., and Loew, H. Z. Social studies and language: A partnership. *Social Education*, 1985, *49*, 92–96.

Burnett, D. G., & Robinson, F. B. Foreign languages and international studies: A consortial approach to institutional development. *ADFL Bulletin*, 1985, *17*, (1), 9–13.

Byrnes, H., & Canale, M. (Eds.). *Defining and developing proficiency: Guidelines, implementations and concepts*. Lincolnwood, IL: National Textbook Company and ACTFL, 1987.

Calvet, L.-J. *Linguistique et colonialisme*. Paris: Payot, 1974.

Cobarrubias, J., & Fishman, J. (Eds.). *Progress in language planning: International perspectives*. Berlin, New York, Amsterdam: Mouton, 1983.

Coffey, B. ESP — English for specific purposes. In Kinsella, V. (Ed.), *Cambridge language surveys, 3*. Cambridge: Cambridge University Press, 1985.

Devens, M. S. Graduate education in foreign languages and literatures: A view from five universities. *ADFL Bulletin*, 1986, *17*, (3), 14–18.

Devens, M. S., & Bennett, N. J. The MLA surveys of foreign language graduate programs, 1984–85. *ADFL Bulletin*, 1986, *17*, (3), 19–27.

Draper, J. B. *State initiatives and activities in foreign languages and international studies*. Washington: Joint National Committee for Languages, 1984–86.

Eastman, C. M. *Language planning: An introduction*. San Francisco: Chandler and Sharp, 1983.

Eddy, P. A. Attitudes toward foreign language study and requirements in American schools and colleges: Results of a national survey. *ADFL Bulletin*, 1979, *11*, (2), 4–9.

Edwards, J. *Language, society and identity*. Oxford and New York: Basil Blackwell, 1985.

Eurich, N. P. *Corporate classrooms: The learning business*. Princeton, NJ: The Carnegie Foundation for the Advancement of Teaching, 1985.

Eveslage, S. A. Retooling for tomorrow's economy with corporate outreach programs. *Educational Record*, 1986, *67*, (2–3), 48–52.

Fishman, J., Cooper, R., & Conrad, A. (Eds.). *The spread of English*. Rowley, MA: Newbury House, 1977.

Fishman, J., Ferguson, C., & Das Gupta, J. (Eds.). *Language problems of developing nations*. New York: Wiley, 1968.

Forster, P. *The Esperanto movement*. Berlin, New York, Amsterdam: Mouton, 1982.

Galloway, V. Public relations: Making an impact. In Phillips, J. K. (Ed.), *Action for the '80s*. Skokie, IL: National Textbook Company and ACTFL, 1981.

Gaudiani, C. Nurturing the ties that bind: Links between foreign language departments and the rest of the post-secondary educational enterprise. In Mead, R. G., Jr. (Ed.), *Foreign languages: Key links in the chain of understanding*. Middlebury, VT: Northeast Conference on the Teaching of Foreign Languages, 1983.

Gaudiani, C., & Herron, C. A. (Eds.). *Strategies for development of foreign language and literature programs.* New York: Modern Language Association of America, 1984.

Geno, T. H. (Ed.). *Foreign language and international studies: Toward cooperation and integration.* Middlebury, VT: Northeast Conference on the Teaching of Foreign Languages, 1981.

Higgs, T. V. Language teaching and the quest for the Holy Grail. In Higgs, T. V. (Ed.), *Teaching for proficiency, the organizing principle.* Lincolnwood, IL: National Textbook Company and ACTFL, 1984.

Hoegl, J. K. Education in the world system: The demand for language and international proficiencies in economic development and national security. *Foreign Language Annals,* 1986, *19,* 281–287.

Hope, G. R., Taylor, H. F., & Pusack, J. P. *Using computers in teaching foreign languages.* Washington, DC: CAL/ERIC, 1984.

Humblet, J.-E. The language problem in international organizations. *International Social Science Journal,* 1984, *36,* 143–155.

Iodice, D. R. Foreign languages and international business: Are we meeting the needs? *ADFL Bulletin,* 1983, *15,* (1), 27–29.

Jolly, G., & Robertson, R. La crise de la langue dans les pays du Commonwealth. In Maurais, J. (Ed.), *La crise des langues.* Quebec: Conseil de la langue française, 1985.

Jorden, E. H. Language and area studies: In search of a meaningful relationship. *ADFL Bulletin,* 1982, *14,* (2), 25–30.

Kennedy, C. (Ed.). *Language planning and language education.* London: Allen and Unwin, 1983.

Kennedy, C. Language planning. In Kinsella, V. (Ed.), *Cambridge language surveys, 3.* Cambridge: Cambridge University Press, 1985.

König, F. H., & Robbins, J. C. The possibilities for interdepartmental cooperation: The experience of two departments. *ADFL Bulletin,* 1984, *15,* (3), 28–30.

Lambert, R. D. *Language and area studies review.* Philadelphia: American Academy of Political and Social Science, 1973.

Lambert, R. D. International studies: An overview and agenda. *Annals of the American Academy of Political and Social Science,* May 1980, *449,* 151–164.

Lambert, R. D. *Beyond growth: The next stage in language and area studies.* Washington, DC: Association of American Universities, 1984.

Laponce, J. A. *Langue et territoire.* Québec: Presses de l'Universite Laval, 1984.

Laroche, J. M. Undergraduate internship in conversation. *Foreign Language Annals,* 1985, *18.*

McCoy, I. H., & Weible, D. M. Foreign languages and the new media: The videodisc and the microcomputer. In James, C. J. (Ed.), *Practical applications of research in foreign language teaching.* Lincolnwood, IL: National Textbook Company and ACTFL.

McDonough, J. *ESP in perspective: A practical guide.* London: Collins, 1984.

Ogden, J. D. *Teaching French as a multilingual language.* Washington, DC: CAL/ERIC, 1981.

Omaggio, A. C. (Ed.). *Proficiency, curriculum articulation: The ties that bind.* Middlebury, VT: Northeast Conference on the Teaching of Foreign Languages, 1985.

Pacqué, R. Deutsche Sprachentscheidungen im politischen Umfeld der Vereinten Nationen. *Multilingua,* 1983, *2,* 19–26.

Patterson, N. Multilingualism in the European Community. *Multilingua,* 1982, *1,* 9–15.

Phillips, J. K. (Ed.). *Action for the '80s: A political, professional, and public program for foreign language education.* Skokie, IL: National Textbook Company and ACTFL, 1981.

Royer, R. G., & McKim, L. W. *PR prototypes: A guidebook for promoting foreign language study to the public.* Washington, DC: CAL/ERIC, 1981.

Strolle, J. M. Comments on communicating with the administration. *ADFL Bulletin,* 1983, *15,* (1), 10–11.

Szepe, G. Less taught languages in Europe (their place in education and their role). Document

ED-80/WS/14. Division of Structures, Content, Methods and Techniques of Education, Unesco, Paris, 1980.

Szerdahelyi, I. Espéranto et propédeutique linguistique. *Langues Modernes*, 1966, *60*, 255–259.

Tollefson, J. W. Language policy and the radical left in the Philippines: The New People's Army and its antecedents. Forthcoming in *Language Problems and Language Planning*, 1986, *10*.

Tonkin, H. Equalizing language. *Journal of Communication*, 1979, *29*, 124–133.

Tonkin, H. Language and international studies: Closing the gap. *ADFL Bulletin*, 1981, *13*, (1), 13–20.

Tonkin, H. Foreign language and the humanities. *ADFL Bulletin*, 1985, *17*, (1), 5–8.

Tonkin, H., & Edwards, J. *The world in the curriculum: Curricular strategies for the 21st century*. New Rochelle, NY: Change Magazine Press, 1981.

Trudgill, P. (Ed.). *Language in the British Isles*. Cambridge: Cambridge University Press, 1984.

Wallach, M. K. Communicating with your community. *ADFL Bulletin*, 1984, *15*, (3), 31–33.

Weinstein, B. Francophonie: A language-based movement in world politics. *International Organization*, 1976, *30*, 485–506.

Weinstein, B. *The civic tongue*. New York: Longman, 1983.

Witkam, A. P. M. *Distributed language translation*. Utrecht: BSO, 1983.

Wood, R. E. Teaching the interlanguage: Some experiments. *Lektos* (University of Louisville), 1975, *Special Issue*, 61–81.

GORDON MACKAY AMBACH was appointed by the State Board of Regents as President of the University of the State of New York and Commissioner of Education July 1, 1977. Prior to that appointment, he served as the Department's Executive Deputy Commissioner from 1970 to 1977. He joined the Department in 1967 as Special Assistant for Long Range Planning to Commissioner James E. Allen, Jr.

The Commissioner's career in the field of education spans a variety of professional teaching and administrative assignments — including teaching at the secondary and university levels and administration in planning, policy development, and management — in state, federal, and local education agencies. His federal assignments have included four years in Washington with the U.S. Office of Education and service under five U.S. Commissioners of Education.

Mr. Ambach was born in Providence, Rhode Island, in 1934 and attended public schools in that city. He graduated from Yale University in 1956 and was awarded a Master of Arts in Teaching from Harvard University in 1957. He serves on the boards of several community and education organizations, and on the local and university committees for both Yale and Harvard universities.

Gordon M. Ambach

Incorporating an International Dimension in Education Reform: Strategies for Success

The New York State Plan for Global Education

A brief historical perspective may be helpful as background for current developments in support of international education. In 1980, staff of the New York State Education Department presented to our Board of Regents a paper summarizing New York State's needs for education in international affairs, foreign languages, and multicultural understanding.[1] The paper placed great emphasis on the need to revive and expand New York's international economic sector as a key prescription to ensure economic health in the future. It also referred to factors in society and in political life which encouraged development of a citizenry informed about international and cultural affairs and equipped with communications skills for capitalizing on the opportunities offered by a changing world.

The paper was under preparation when the President's Commission on Foreign Language and International Studies made its recommendations in its report *Strength Through Wisdom* (November, 1979).[2] The extensive media coverage afforded the Commission's findings helped to stimulate public support for the two fundamental goals of the Education for a Global Perspective plan: (1) to develop among all students a knowledge and understanding of the cultures of this nation and the world, and (2) to provide more students with communication skills necessary to meet their personal, academic, and professional objectives in both their own and other cultural settings and languages.

The President's Commission accentuated those movements toward change which were apparent in state and local agencies several years before. "Global Education"—a somewhat ambiguous title—became the subject of many studies, conferences, and workshops from the mid-seventies onward. At the same time, arising from different forces within American society, a parallel movement developed, known as "Multicultural Education." Global education, in addition to teaching about interdependence, included the study of peoples and cultures around the world, while multicultural education focused on educating America's young for a pluralistic society in which many cultures could exist together within the American democracy.

Both movements recognized the necessity for precollegiate students to learn how to behave with persons from cultures unlike their own. These behavioral objectives re-

quired the development of skills which had, for the most part, been neglected in a heavily
cognitive and systematically deductive educational methodology. To learn about another
culture one must largely leave behind one's preconceptions, prejudices, and biases, using
less familiar inductive learning techniques. Whether the goal is ethnic or racial understanding at home or international understanding abroad, the method is the same.

At the same time, the economic success of other nations, particularly the Japanese,
suggested that the United States needed to take a fresh look at how foreign languages
were taught and learned. In 1981, the Council on Learning reported that, while 90 percent of all college students had at one time studied a language, only 33 percent felt
that they could order a meal in that language and only 8 percent could understand
a native speaker of the language.

Enrollments in Regents-Examination-level foreign language courses in New York State
had dropped from 48 percent in 1969 to 35.2 percent in 1979. Secondary school language enrollments dropped as college entrance requirements eliminated the foreign
language requirements. In New York State many students in grades 9–12 continued
to study foreign languages; however, the incentives for continuation became less at-
tractive as the college requirements diminished.

It was thus in a climate of growing dissatisfaction with the inadequacy of global
education, foreign language and multicultural education programs at all levels and at
a time of international crisis in Afghanistan, Iran, and elsewhere, that the paper, "Education for a Global Perspective," was presented to the Board of Regents in December
1980.

INTEGRATION WITH COMPREHENSIVE EDUCATION REFORM

At the same time that the Plan for Education for a Global Perspective was being
developed and given broad review by interested parties, several other important policy
reviews were also being conducted by the Education Department and the Board of
Regents. These included a review of Education for Civic Values, Integrating the Arts
into Education, review and change of physical education requirements, of guidance
requirements, and of curricula and syllabi in many subjects. Over a period of two and
a half years beginning in 1981, these and other efforts were drawn into a comprehensive
examination of goals and actions for elementary and secondary education in New York
State. This process began with a restatement of Regents Goals for Elementary and
Secondary School students (previously revised ten years earlier in 1974), and then moved
to a detailed plan spelling out the actions schools can and must take to help students
meet those goals. This plan, which I advanced to the Regents and is formally known
as the Regents Action Plan to Improve Elementary and Secondary Education Results
in New York State, was adopted in final form in March 1984.[3]

The Regents Goals Project, culminating in the adoption of the Action Plan, provided extensive opportunities for involvement by the widest possible range of constituents, representing both the educational and the business sectors within the state. The
broad participation by school administrators, teachers, members of local school boards,
parents, students, and business people was extremely important in achieving a better
understanding through a shared ownership of expectations affecting all those who have
a part in or are affected by the implementation of change. At the same time, the Board
of Regents incorporated the new educational goals outlined in the concurrently developed
specific plans.

IMPLEMENTATION

In November 1984, the Board of Regents approved the Commissioner's Regulations which raise the standards in virtually all areas of elementary and secondary education. For all practical purposes, these new regulations are synonymous with the Action Plan.

One of the most significant and certainly most widely discussed aspects of the regulations is that they change the status of second language education from an elective to a required subject. Specifically, the new regulations provide that all public school students first entering grade nine in 1988 and 1989 must complete at least one year of study in a language other than English at some time during grades kindergarten through nine. All public school students who first enter grade nine in 1990 and thereafter must complete two years of second language study at some time during grades kindergarten through nine. In addition, students who wish to earn a Regents high school diploma (a credential requiring completion of a more demanding course of study and examinations) must earn at least three Carnegie units of credit in a single second language and pass a statewide Regents comprehensive examination in that language. Since, under certain conditions, students may earn one unit of credit toward a high school diploma for the successful completion of their *early* second language learning requirement, Regents diploma recipients will have completed at least four years of second language study by the time they graduate from high school. Some students may conclude their program with as many as six years of second language study by meeting elective course requirements in a language other than English.

The Action Plan resulted also in either additional or new requirements in mathematics, science, social studies, art, and music, as well as occupational education subjects. It is noteworthy that many of the recommendations of the Education for a Global Perspective plan were incorporated in the revised statement of Regents Goals, the Action Plan, and the related Commissioner's Regulations. For example, there are relevant goals and subgoals under seven of the ten goals included in the Goals statement.

Specific course requirements, syllabus revisions, examination changes, and other strategies of the Education for a Global Perspective plan were also infused throughout the Regents Action Plan. Although the new Action Plan became effective on September 1, 1985, implementation of the various parts of the Plan will actually occur over the coming decade. This is true, also, of those aspects related to international and multicultural education and particularly of the increased second language requirements. I consider this especially important from a strategic point of view because it assures an orderly phase-in and allows time for development of the resources necessary to achieve our goals.

We are uniquely fortunate in New York State to have *all* levels and sectors of education within one comprehensive system: The University of the State of New York. From the beginning, therefore, our Plan included strategies to be followed by elementary and secondary schools, colleges and universities, and cultural education institutions (museums, libraries, public radio and television stations). In other states, coordination of these education sectors might require a more aggressive effort of the state education agency, the governor, or the institutions themselves, perhaps assisted by the several constituent representative organizations.

Our Plan laid out very specific steps to be taken by our State Education Department, the schools, higher education institutions, and cultural education institutions.

Schools. The schools are charged with implementing changes in syllabi, materials, and examinations; with supplementing inservice training; and with selecting languages for both elementary and secondary level instruction based not only on community needs but also on state and national needs and interests.

Higher education institutions. Colleges and universities play a crucial role in the preparation of common-branch teachers with second language proficiency and of foreign language teachers directed toward new curricular goals; in the establishment of graduate level centers for the study of both language and culture, especially in the "critical languages" not commonly taught in the schools (Russian, Chinese, Arabic, Japanese, etc.).

In order to be "broad and broad-based," a plan for international (or global) education must reach into almost every subject area in the schools. For example, as noted above, our Plan affects instruction in social studies, arts and humanities, science (particularly with reference to global environmental and ecological issues), business education, bilingual education, and foreign languages.

Under our Regents Action Plan, all students will take a two-year sequence in global studies in the ninth and tenth grades. This year's sixth-grade students will have completed two units of study of a second language by the end of ninth grade, and a three-unit language sequence to receive a high school diploma. In addition to course requirements, our Plan has "check-points" on performance: an elementary level social studies examination, two high school level social studies exams, and three levels of foreign language tests.

We are developing new examinations in foreign language teaching to reflect the changed instructional approach which emphasizes "functional proficiency"—that is, greater stress on oral (speaking and listening) skills. New draft syllabi for language instruction have also been prepared and distributed to the schools.

Action at the National Level

In November 1984, I was privileged to be elected President of the Council of Chief State School Officers (CCSSO), the coordinating organization of the Commissioners of Education, Superintendents of Instruction, and like officials of the 50 states and the territories.

Recognizing the growing national concern for the competitive position of our nation in the global economy, the CCSSO set the theme of international dimensions of education for its annual meeting in November 1985. Over the course of that year, the Council developed a position paper and recommendations for action. This paper also was prepared with extensive consultation with experts in the field and affected groups. The Council members reviewed and adopted the paper unanimously at their meeting at EPCOT Center in Florida, a meeting attended also by ministers of education from a number of other nations.

The November 1985 paper, "International Dimensions of Education,"[4] reiterates the long-standing commitment of CCSSO to the issues. More importantly, it presents a course of action for the Council, federal agencies, and the several states in order to better realize that commitment.

The CCSSO paper notes four basic facets of the international dimensions of education. First is skill in *communications*, the capacity to communicate in languages other than English. Second, is knowledge about and understanding of nations, cultures, and people other than our own, and the worldwide issues which must be addressed — *international education*. The third dimension of international education is the capacity to *compare educational systems* and results across national boundaries. Fourth, is the capacity to help nations learn from one another about their solutions to common educational challenges — *the exchange of educational practices*. These four aspects are further described as follows:

1 **Communication skills.** All American students should have the opportunity to learn a language other than English. The opportunity should include study in languages other than European languages, and should begin in the earliest years of elementary school with continuation through the post-secondary level. Students completing secondary school should be able to demonstrate an acceptable level of proficiency in communications, particularly speaking and listening, in a language other than English.

   Study of a second language provides students not only with the ability to communicate effectively across nations and cultures, but also to understand other cultures through their languages, gain insight into the structure of language, and acquire skill for employment.

   To assure effective language learning, teachers of second languages should have firsthand experience in the cultures of the languages they teach. Exchanges of middle school and secondary school students among nations should be expanded. Students unable to experience such an exchange should have experiences through contact within their communities with exchange students, native-speaking foreign nationals, and use of telecommunications.

2 **International Education.** International Education is both the formal approach to study of the world — its history and geography, its peoples and their languages and cultures, its economic systems, its political and social systems — and an interdisciplinary approach to global issues such as the environment, energy, conflict resolution, resource allocation, and human rights.

3 **Cross-national comparisons of educational data.** Cross-national comparisons of education are necessary to understand our own and other cultures and to assess use of different educational practices. Collaborative efforts among federal agencies, states, and international education associations must be developed and strengthened to promote cooperation for high quality collection, exchange, and interpretation of comparative data.

4 **Exchange of educational practices.** Educational practitioners in the United States need to have access to information on programs, projects, and individual efforts in other countries that suggest successful methods for addressing issues or problems at the local, regional, or national level. International networks should be established to exchange compatible educational practices and materials that can bring new life and quality to existing school programs and provide innovative approaches to educational problems. By joint sponsorship of international conferences and exchange of strategies on topics such as youth transition from school to work, urban education, early childhood education, and second language study, educators through the world can learn and adapt from the best each nation has achieved.

The recommendations for action included in the position paper are directed toward different levels of government and institutions or organizations, grouped under six rubrics: Council activities; federal agencies; CCSSO and federal agencies; state education agencies; local education agencies; state education agencies, colleges, and universities. From the total of 43 recommendations, those of particular interest to readers of the Northeast Conference *Reports* and others involved in foreign language instruction appear as Appendix A.

Elements of Successful Collaboration

The Education for a Global Perspective plan was indeed the first direct step leading to the formulation of second language study requirements as an integral part of a general redesign of educational programs at the elementary and secondary school levels in New York State. For that reason, a review of the most critical elements which contributed to the success of the plan may be of special interest to foreign language educators.

Viewed in retrospect, the plan's success in helping achieve the results described above depended largely on a perfect mix of a number of equally important elements. Good timing from beginning to end was one of them. As has been indicated, the concluding phases of the Education for a Global Perspective plan coincided with the early phases in formulating the Regents Action Plan. This timing led to the integration of the Global Perspective goals (one of them being the strengthening of second language programs) into the overall goals for elementary and secondary education. At any other time, the idea of preparing students for life in an interdependent world might have gone the way of so many other well-intentioned and well-articulated "position papers."

Although launched independently and based on New York State's needs as a world trade, information, service, manufacturing, financial, and cultural center, the Education for a Global Perspective plan made a strong initial impact with the aid of concurrent discussions at the national level about "our gross national inadequacy in foreign language skills," as had been charged by the President's Commission on Foreign Language and International Studies.

Another important element in the evolution of the second language mandate was its relationship to broader educational concerns. It has been mentioned before that it did not occur in isolation. Beginning with the Education for a Global Perspective plan, the second language issue was always discussed as one of several imperatives relative to preparing students for life in a world one must view as a network of interdependent cultural, social, economic, political, and environmental systems, a world which requires skills for understanding one's own values, beliefs, and attitudes and those of other cultures, and, consequently, the ability to communicate effectively not only in English, but in at least one other language. Placing the need for second language learning in a broader context helped to foster public understanding and support.

One very important element for our success was the fit between the objectives of the Global Perspective plan and our New York State's long-standing commitment to bilingual education. We recognized that students and teachers in bilingual programs are a great "natural resource" to help us meet the goals of multilingual and multicultural education for all students in New York, and to develop a truly bilingual population.

Critical also was the role played by the state's foreign language teacher organizations in various phases of the project, especially with regard to promoting second language education by means of a well-coordinated public awareness campaign. At about the same time the Board of Regents instructed the State Education Department staff to develop a plan for addressing global education needs, the New York State Association of Foreign Language Teachers, in conjunction with the Classical Association of the Empire State, developed a video program which demonstrated the values and benefits of second language learning.[5] Intended for the general public, the program featured leading representatives of business and industry who spoke about the importance of second language competence in manufacturing and commerce. When the program was aired over the State's public educational television network, the professional language teacher associations invited members of other educational organizations as well as business and ethnic groups to view and discuss the program at viewing centers especially organized for that purpose. In short, the State's foreign language teacher organizations assumed a major part in sustaining continued public awareness of global education issues. These efforts were absolutely essential in mobilizing support for and neutralizing opposition to the Regents Plan for Education for a Global Perspective and the Regents Action Plan.

The professional organizations' strong support of the Education for a Global Perspective plan and, subsequently, the Goals Project and Action Plan implies, of course, that the Board of Regents and State Education Department's policy was acceptable to those who would be most directly affected by the policy. The consistency of state policy with the aims and objectives of the professional organizations is extremely important if the policy is to be implemented successfully. It is best achieved through direct involvement of organization leaders in the policy-making process.

There is no single formula for mechanisms that provide for interaction between policy makers and constituents. Based on the recommendations of the President's Commission on Foreign Language and International Studies, some states have established advisory councils to discuss relevant issues and to develop strategies for addressing those issues. In New York State there was no need to establish such councils because of existing channels of communication. In fact, frequent interaction between State Education Department staff and the professional organizations has been a way of life for a long period of time.

At one level, the State Education Department's subject specialists (called "consultants" in some states), have very close and cordial working relationships with the statewide organizations which represent teachers in their respective subject areas. These relationships exist as a result of professional courtesy and the need to get things done effectively and efficiently. When practiced continuously and judiciously, this kind of relationship tends to foster mutual understanding and trust and obviates the need for *ad hoc* committees and advisory councils.

Although the concept of a global perspective plan was explored initially by a committee consisting solely of State Education Department personnel, the views and concerns of foreign language teachers as well as other constituents were expressed and considered at all times by Department staff. Throughout the process, these staff members were in contact with the leaders of the statewide organizations, providing and discussing information about the progress of the project. At the same time, the Department staff obtained reactions and suggestions from rank-and-file members channeled through the organizations' statewide communication network. This interaction was critical in the development of realistic goals and objectives for foreign language and international studies. It also provided opportunities for teachers, through their professional organizations working closely with State Education Department subject specialists, to be involved in the formulation of policy.

At another level, interaction is fostered by the accessibility of top policy makers to the professional teacher organizations. Associations representing foreign language teachers in New York State have been particularly active in cultivating discussion with members of the Board of Regents, the Commissioner of Education, and members of the State Legislature by inviting them frequently to participate actively in statewide and regional meetings and conferences. This strategy has been of mutual benefit because (1) it helped policy makers focus on issues related to foreign language and international studies, and (2) it provided foreign language educators with the broader educational context which is of primary concern to policy makers.

Once a policy has been established, professional organizations must continue to play a vital role in assuring that the policy succeeds. The nature of this role will depend upon the personnel and material resources available. The tasks performed should complement rather than duplicate activities which the state education agency undertakes. A close cooperation between these entities is, again, highly desirable.

The importance of an effective public awareness campaign, produced and carried out by foreign language teacher organizations, has already been discussed. Through publications and regional meetings these organizations also have established a network of communication with their constituents which is being used extensively by State Education Department personnel to review and explain all the details of the new regulations with respect to second language requirements. The organizations thus provide vital service in the dissemination of information among constituents at all instructional levels.

Foreign language teacher organizations, through their representatives, are also important participants in two of the most critical aspects of the implementation of the Regents Action Plan: curriculum and staff development. Members of the profession, including staff of the American Council on the Teaching of Foreign Languages (ACTFL), have provided valuable advice and assistance to our Department in all stages of developing our new syllabi for modern languages and Latin. Many of the same persons are now involved in the delivery of staff development activities designed to acquaint all teachers with the new syllabi and strategies for implementing them. Professional organizations have unique capabilities for assessing teachers' inservice training needs and identifying individuals who have specific experience and expertise in meeting those needs. These capabilities are being used effectively in planning teacher workshops at regional meetings and conferences.

Given the existence of other factors, such as good timing and a general climate conducive to reorganizing priorities, individuals in the educational community, through the organizations which represent them, have not only an opportunity but also an obligation to participate in the process of bringing about change. Based on our experience in New York State, best results are achieved if the involvement of professional organizations in the making and implementation of educational policy is the result of continuous, rather than sporadic, interaction with those who have statutory responsibility for setting that policy. The state's foreign language supervisor/coordinator can play an important role as both facilitator and, when needed, buffer in that relationship. The nature of the relationship will dictate what specific role the professional organizations will assume. In New York State, the organizations have concentrated on (1) mobilizing support for foreign language studies through public awareness campaigns and cultivating alliances with other potential spokespersons representing the interests of business, industry, commerce, and ethnic groups; (2) participation in and dissemination of information about statewide curriculum projects; and (3) improving instruction through intensive staff development programs.

Initiatives to promote and strengthen foreign language education at the local and state levels are important steps in the right direction.

In some cases, these initiatives may build on programs created as actions to improve the overall quality of teaching. For example, in New York State, the Legislature and the Governor in 1984 approved, at the request of the Board of Regents, a program of Empire State Scholarships and Fellowships for Teachers. The original subject areas were mathematics and science. In 1986, the name was changed to Empire State Challenger Scholarships and Fellowships, to honor the memory of the astronauts who died in the space shuttle Challenger; and the program was expanded to include bilingual education, teachers of English to Speakers of Other Languages, and foreign languages, as well as certain other subjects identified as shortage areas. The program provides 312 undergraduate scholarships and 650 graduate fellowships, each with a required teaching obligation. This program might be a model for replication in other states.[6]

However, given the need for all Americans to be able to communicate in languages other than English in order to compete successfully at the international marketplace, it is imperative that these efforts be supported philosophically and financially at the national level.

I know that the Council of Chief State School Officers would welcome the partnership of national organizations serving foreign language teachers in achieving its goals set forth for international dimensions of education. The selected list of these goals provided in Appendix A suggests an extensive agenda to realize the potential of the international dimensions of education. Teachers, through their professional organizations, must work closely with state education agencies and with other constituencies with an interest in foreign languages and international education to develop a common agenda which *all* can support. This process will require a spirit of flexibility. Moving forward in a spirit of cooperation and collaboration, we can do much to achieve our mutual goals.

Appendix A

**Selected Recommendations from the CCSSO Position Paper
on International Dimensions of Education (November 1985)**

COUNCIL ACTIONS

- Provide leadership in working with states to improve the quality of second language study and teaching of international education. In particular, the Council should identify talent and resources; arrange connections with the Department of Commerce and civic, business, and professional groups; and support curriculum development, teacher training, public information, and evaluation of projects.

- Create a national forum with professional education associations involved in international education and second language study to further program collaboration and information dissemination on a national level.

- Join with federal or international agencies to establish cooperative assessment and evaluation programs of state and local international education and second language initiatives.

- Work with colleges, universities, and educational organizations to review second language entrance and graduation requirements, availability of courses in infrequently taught languages, and standards for teacher preparation and certification related to international education and second languages.

TO FEDERAL AGENCIES

• Propose federal legislation for comprehensive assistance to international education and second language study at the elementary and secondary level. This legislation should provide incentives to:

  a encourage states to serve as coordinators of intercultural and international activities in cooperation with various United States government and private agencies.

  b provide funding for state and local program planning, curriculum development, and special programs that include:

    1 the development of evaluation and assessment systems and validated tests

    2 in-service and pre-service training of personnel in international studies and second languages

    3 state and local links with counterpart agencies in other nations

    4 community/citizen exchange programs

    5 international exchange programs for education personnel and students, including school to school exchanges

    6 establishing or expanding centers or special international high schools for the study of second languages or international studies in each state

  c encourage the use of telecommunication, computer and videodisc technologies for teaching a second language in areas where foreign language teachers are in short supply and for the less commonly taught languages.

  d encourage state and local provision for study in the less commonly taught languages of Russian, Japanese, Portuguese, Arabic, and Chinese.

• Strengthen research programs within federally funded regional laboratories and centers to promote research and its dissemination in comparative educational data and practices, second language study and international perspectives in curriculum. Topics of research should include methods of second language study; use of learning technologies; and comparative studies of student achievement, knowledge, and attitudes.

• Establish a National Fund for International Education to provide support for international education initiatives, including international exchange of scholars, educators, and students as well as support for collaborative efforts in educational data collection and research. This Fund should receive a portion of reflow funds and *encourage contributions abroad from United States firms unable to repatriate profits.* U.S. tax deductions should be permitted on contributions made to the Fund abroad by their foreign subsidiaries.

• Expand availability of other nations' media programs and broadcasts for international education and second language study using satellites and other communication technologies. Multi-national efforts should include attention to copyright restrictions related to news and government operations.

TO STATE EDUCATION AGENCIES

• Work with state boards of education to review or establish policy statements on improving and expanding the international dimensions of education.

• Provide leadership in working with local education agencies (LEAs) to improve the quality of second language teaching and learning and provide an international perspective in existing studies. These initiatives should include the following:

a surveying existing talent and resources within the state and assessing need;

b developing curriculum with an international perspective in geography, history, social sciences, second languages, mathematics, sciences and the arts; preparing an evaluation framework for programs; and planning for personnel training and public information;

c encouraging addition of the less commonly taught languages to school offerings;

d engaging business, civic, and professional groups and other state agencies having international concerns (commerce, agriculture) in the support of international education

• Encourage participation in international exchange programs by administrators, teachers, and students.

• Expand the use of America's ethnic and linguistic minorities, foreign students, returned Peace Corps volunteers, and other Americans having extensive experience abroad in second language teaching and international education.

• Provide a focus on international education and study of second languages through state assessment and data collection systems. Establish teacher certification and accreditation procedures so that second language teachers demonstrate a high level of language proficiency and teaching ability, as well as a knowledge of the people, history and institutions of the nation(s) or region in which the language is spoken.

• Require LEAs to provide the opportunity for all students to study a second language, introducing these opportunities at the elementary school level where possible.

• Establish expectations and proficiency goals in second languages for students completing high school.

• Establish regular school year and summer programs for students focusing on second languages or international issues in business, economics, environment, and government.

• Work with various levels of the education system (elementary, secondary, college, technical instruction, and university) to integrate instruction so that international education and second language study are well-connected among levels and each student's learning is continuous.

• Establish procedures for granting academic credit for study abroad experience at accredited institutions and create expanded opportunities for required testing in overseas locations.

TO LOCAL EDUCATION AGENCIES

• Adopt policies and support programs designed to strengthen second language study and international education. Review tests and assessment programs to ensure that international dimensions are adequately considered.

• Provide teachers and other professionals opportunities to participate in exchange and in-service programs that improve their competence in second languages.

• Provide every student with opportunity to begin the study of a second language in the earliest years of formal education and to continue study of the language until a functional proficiency has been achieved. Local school districts are encouraged to identify students with high aptitude for language study and provide opportunity for these students to pursue advanced study, in regular or special schools, such as "international high schools" and to offer opportunities to live and study in other nations. Local education agencies are encouraged to offer uncommonly taught languages (Arabic, Chinese, Japanese, Portuguese, and Russian).

TO STATE EDUCATION AGENCIES, COLLEGES, AND UNIVERSITIES

• Urge colleges and universities to establish (or reinstate) second language requirements for admission to and graduation from appropriate post-secondary programs. The requirements should include demonstrated proficiency in speaking, listening, reading, and writing the language, not solely the earning of credit hours of second language study. Institutions can be guided in setting levels of proficiency by national standards developed by language specialists.

• Include as part of preparation for teaching a second language study in a nation or area where that language is primary. State education agencies, colleges, and universities should collaborate in establishing requirements for this study as part of teacher preparation and certification.

• Allow students to utilize financial resources/scholarships for overseas study opportunities for a limited period.

Notes

1 "Education for a Global Perspective." Position paper of the New York State Board of Regents. Albany, NY, New York State Education Department, 1980.

2 *Strength Through Wisdom: A Critique of U.S. Capability.* Report of the President's Commission on Foreign Language and International Studies. Washington, DC, Superintendent of Documents, 1979.

3 *New York State Board of Regents Action Plan to Improve Elementary and Secondary Education Results in New York.* Albany, NY, New York State Education Department, March 1984.

4 *International Dimensions of Education.* Position paper and recommendations for action. Washington, DC, Council of Chief State School Officers, November 1985.

5 "Changing World." Videotape available for $75 from Center for Learning Technologies, New York State Education Department, Albany, NY 12230, Attn: William Humphrey. Teacher Guide ($10) available from New York State Association of Foreign Language Teachers, 1102 Ardsley Road, Schenectady, NY 12308.

6 Application forms and information available at any school or college in New York State or directly from: Bureau of Higher and Professional Education Testing, Room 5C64, Cultural Education Center, Albany, NY 12230.

ALICE G. PINDERHUGHES is Superintendent of Baltimore City Public Schools. A graduate of New York University, Mrs. Pinderhughes has spent all of her professional career in the Baltimore Public Schools beginning as an elementary school teacher before becoming an elementary principal, then elementary supervisor, and subsequently assistant superintendent. She has been superintendent since 1983.

She has devoted much of her professional career to early childhood education. She organized the Early Childhood Education Area in Baltimore and acted as project manager for the nationally acclaimed Model Early Childhood Education Program that received the President's Pacesetter Award.

Mrs. Pinderhughes is the recipient of four honorary degrees and has served or is currently serving on the boards of several professional organizations. As the leader of one of the country's largest urban school systems, she has transformed the curriculum of the Baltimore City Public Schools into an internationally oriented curriculum with a strong foreign language component. Her leadership in this area is nationally recognized.

Alice G. Pinderhughes

Baltimore's Foreign Language Mandate: An Experiment That Works

Background and Rationale

When we decided to implement a program to teach foreign language to every child in grades six, seven, and eight in the Baltimore City Public Schools, even some of our ardent supporters indicated that this might not be our most prudent decision. On the evidence, I can sympathize with their misgivings.

I administer one of the largest school systems in the country. Last year we had approximately 113,000 students, more than 70 percent non-white, and approximately 12 percent absent from school on any given day. In the course of the year, we knew that about 11 percent, no matter how hard we tried, would drop out, ending their formal schooling prematurely. In our nine zoned high schools, more than half the students were not reading and computing on grade level. Why, then, would any sane, experienced, committed educator think that foreign language instruction would serve the interests of all of our young adolescents who are not learning disabled?

My training and experience lie, primarily, in the area of elementary education. I am acutely aware of the way in which young children process and master language. For the most part, language skills grow through imitation, through practice, and through reinforcement. Consequently, the scamp who can do a brilliant impersonation of Miss Figg, down to her intonations and syntactical peculiarities, can imitate Miss Figg's French accent and vocabulary, given the motivation and skilled teaching. The fact that a child is reading a grade below his current placement may be totally irrelevant.

Moreover, it is our experience that the older children are when a new language is introduced, the greater the likelihood that they will be inhibited about communicating through unfamiliar sounds. Since primary language is *oral* language, we can presume that our youngsters aged 12 to 14 will be freer of the social queasiness which impedes the adult language student.

In addition, I am convinced that we must offer our children the possibility of learning a fairly broad menu of disciplines. If we do not offer inner-city children the possibility of speaking French or Spanish, their parents and their life experiences aren't apt to open the doors. We have to whet appetites if the material is to be tasted.

Finally, there is a more distant, perhaps more profound reason for our attempt to offer foreign language study to so many middle school youngsters. I believe that communication is the only defense we have against injustice, violence, subjugation, and all manner of political absurdity. We must be able to talk to others from distant lands and alien cultures. We must be able to listen and to understand what we are told. Communication, ultimately, may save our lives.

What Was Our Mandate?

Today the Baltimore City Public Schools are in the fifth year of a unique and successful foreign language initiative, the foreign language mandate. Over 30,000 of this urban school district's 113,000 students are enrolled in some component of a program of required and sequential language study. Students in ten of the city's elementary schools study French or Spanish in grades four and five as part of a pilot elementary program. All students enrolled in the system's middle schools are required to study French or Spanish in grades six, seven, and eight. All ninth-grade students must continue the study of their middle school foreign language for a year and college preparatory students must continue their language study through grade 12.

In addition to the primary mandated languages, French and Spanish, students may elect programs of study that include Latin, German, and Japanese.

The realization of the mandate for expanded foreign language instruction required a broad collaborative effort. Parents, curriculum supervisors, central office administrators, university faculty, the mayor's office, teachers, community representatives, and the state department of education worked together to support the project.

Under our administrative design, we are governed by a policy-making board of school commissioners which had to be intensely involved in the development of the new language instruction model. Fundamental decisions were involved because the program clearly required redeployment of resources and revision of the students' scheduled school day. In fact, one of our commissioners was the spark who ignited the initial change.

How Was the Board Involved in the Innovation?

The foreign language mandate ultimately received the approval of all nine school commissioners. It should be noted, however, that the endorsement came only after the rigorous analysis required for such a major innovation.

A prominent issue considered throughout the initial stages of the approval process was the question: Why is it important to have a systematic foreign language mandate for *all* students? The board was impressed by arguments describing the cognitive benefits of foreign language study. Through a series of staff and consultants' presentations, the board studied the probability of verbal skill enhancement and improvement of SAT scores through foreign language study. In addition, the board reviewed the value of foreign language study as a key to opening up to students literature, art, music, and lifestyles from other cultures. The board concluded that the case for foreign languages rested on its own laurels. National studies such as *The Carnegie Task Force on Teaching as a Profession*, the report of the Paideia Group, *A Nation at Risk*, as well as the research have supported the value of foreign language study.

After deliberation, our board unanimously approved the new foreign language mandate. In doing so, board members were aware of their pioneering role. They also realized that a long range view should be taken; it would take five to ten years for us to evaluate the ultimate impact of the mandate on student achievement. We saw this initiative as one segment of our total effort to improve students' achievement; other elements include: explicit teaching of thinking skills, study skills instruction, revision of required programs to make content more rigorous, and the use of business partnerships to enrich curricular possibilities. Our school system has had the good fortune to be associated closely with people in business and industry who have an understanding of the importance of foreign language study.

In summary, our board has held two primary views related to this issue: (1) Board members should be concerned that students comprehend world history and international events involving major world powers. Requiring more foreign language study of all students enhances our American awareness of other cultures. (2) Our review of the literature has shown that the earlier foreign language study the better. We see such study as essential in equipping our students for life in the twenty-first century.

How Does the Curriculum Accomplish the Mandate?

The goal of the Baltimore City foreign language program is to provide a sequential program of study that can lead to the development of communicative competence. The program, which has been developed cooperatively by foreign language educators, is based on communications goals which were drafted by teachers and supervisory staff.

Our foreign language program extends from elementary through senior high school. At the elementary level, fourth-, fifth-, and elementary school-housed sixth-graders attend language classes on an every-other-day basis. Classes last from twenty to thirty minutes. During the three years of elementary study we expect students to accomplish the goals of the level I program. The elementary program is a pilot serving approximately 3,500 students. Teachers assigned to this program generally instruct students in two schools.

At the middle school level foreign language study is required in grades six, seven, and eight. Middle school students study foreign language on alternating days and complete the equivalent of three semesters of instruction during the three years. Students are expected to complete the level I program by the end of their middle school experience. Those students who have already studied language at the elementary program may be placed, at the teacher's recommendation, in classes that can allow them to complete the level II program.

At the high school level, all students with the exception of those who have already enrolled in vocational-technical programs must complete a full year of language study. Those students enrolled in the college preparatory program must continue their study of language. In some of our high schools, principals exercise the option of requiring an additional year of language study for many non-college-bound students.

The language program is assisted by a cadre of in-school and central office support staff. In schools with a large department (four teachers or more), a language department head provides leadership and support in conjunction with assigned central office staff. All schools receive the services of the Office of Foreign Languages supervisor and its two educational specialists.

Carefully supervised innovation and creativity are stressed in the development and use of instructional materials throughout the program. At the elementary level, because of the lack of published texts and because of the emphasis on listening and speaking, teachers create most of their own materials. Middle school teachers make use of a variety of text series. They are encouraged to adapt texts to their own situations. An option at this level is to use no text at all. Senior high school staffs are also encouraged to adapt the texts that their students use.

When we issued the directive to staff to implement this very ambitious and fairly complex program of studies, it did not evoke universal joy. In fact, principals complained about scheduling problems, staff shortages, materials inadequacy, and space limitations. There was more frustration than applause.

What Steps Were Taken to Implement the Program?

One central office administrator, working with the principals and the supervisor of foreign languages, was responsible for implementing the program in our 26 intermediate and 17 senior high schools. Approximately 30,000 students and 165 foreign language teachers were involved in foreign language study in the fall of 1985. This number included both the mandated program in French and Spanish and courses in other languages: German, Japanese, and Latin. In addition, the program has been gradually implemented in ten elementary schools.

It is not hard to imagine some of the problems encountered in implementing a foreign language mandate in such a large number of schools. Although strong support had been indicated at the school board level and from many groups in the community, the logistics of implementing the program posed problems in staffing, scheduling, teacher training, instructional materials, evaluating student progress, space allocation, and financial resources. Despite this long list of issues, staff remained committed to implementation of the mandate as it had been approved by the policy makers.

A review of some of the major obstacles which we had to confront may be helpful to those who would attempt similar projects. Each issue is described, of course, in capsule form.

STAFFING

Perhaps the biggest hurdle faced was that of locating qualified teachers of French and Spanish. While our prime concern was facility with the language, we were also interested in people who had a genuine concern for working with urban youth. In keeping with the foreign language mandate, teachers have been expected to emphasize the communicative function of language at all levels of instruction.

Last year approximately 38 percent of our foreign language teachers were either probationary — that is, they had fewer than three years of experience, or provisional — that is, they had some course or experience deficits. We have been fortunate to have a devoted corps of excellent experienced teachers who provide stability in our program. Still, a pervasive problem in implementing and maintaining a quality program has been the loss of staff. Teachers have left our system for a variety of reasons: maternity, marriage, relocation, graduate studies, economic pressures, career change, and various others.

As the 1986–87 school year began, we projected a foreign language teacher vacancy rate of approximately five percent. One innovative approach which we tried in 1985–86 was that of "importing" European teachers. We have mixed reactions to this approach since we hired four teachers, two of whom have not succeeded and two of whom are planning to remain with us for a second year. We are exploring the possibility of hiring teachers with a strong language background but lacking certification. We are working with staff at the Maryland State Department of Education to investigate and possibly implement this approach as a pilot project. Hiring and maintaining adequate numbers of highly qualified foreign language teachers remains a major dilemma.

STAFF DEVELOPMENT

We work zealously to see that our language teachers are trained in the latest teaching methodologies and are kept abreast of recent trends and developments in the field.

Outside consultants such as Professor John Rassias of Dartmouth and Professor June Phillips of Indiana University of Pennsylvania have provided a continuing program of staff development. We are particularly proud of the involvement of Professor Rassias in our staff development activities, since his highly innovative method has been well received by both our experienced and our novice teachers. Over the last few years, he has provided intensive two- and three-day staff development sessions for our teachers. His approach has influenced classrooms throughout our school system.

During the past year, we have been fortunate to have the services of June Phillips as a leader of several staff development sessions in the area of foreign language oral proficiency. We believe that a major objective of our program is to help students reach higher levels of proficiency; our teachers are being trained in both teaching and testing for proficiency.

Many of our French and Spanish teachers have participated in a multi-year project funded by a grant from the National Endowment for the Humanities to the University of Maryland–Baltimore County. Staff members have participated in intensive immersion training during the summer. A major goal of that program is enhanced teacher proficiency in understanding and speaking French and Spanish. In the past, our teachers have often participated in this program in order to strengthen their command of a second foreign language. A vigorous, progressive program of staff development has been a priority during the initial years of implementing the mandate.

SCHEDULING

Since September 1982, those elementary students who study either French or Spanish in fourth and fifth grades have met on alternate days. In middle schools, students study either French or Spanish for three years following the A-day/B-day (alternate day) scheduling model. All ninth-grade general curriculum and college preparatory students continue their foreign language study daily. Special education pupils may study a foreign language when this is included in the child's Individual Educational Program (IEP). Only college preparatory students are required to study a foreign language in grades 10 through 12.

Our most perplexing problem remains the daily inclusion of foreign language study in the intermediate school schedule. Our original plan required us to schedule more than 400 students per week per teacher. Financial constraints required us to limit the number of staff hired to implement the mandate. During the past several years, the alternate day scheduling pattern has caused problems which many administrators and teachers identify. Most frequently mentioned are the following: inconsistency of instruction, oppressive paperwork, excessive student load, students' confusion regarding the schedule, and general teacher fatigue. We have recently, by board action, modified the mandate to eliminate A-day/B-day scheduling.

RECOMMENDATIONS

We hope that insights gained in the Baltimore City Public Schools' experience will be beneficial to others. Our recommendations for those interested in initiating a foreign language mandate program include:

1 Establish a long sequence for foreign language study, preferably three or more years in order to improve students' mastery of a language.
2 Avoid alternate day scheduling.
3 Establish procedures for evaluating the success of the students and the program.
4 Provide a program of innovative staff development activities designed to respond to the needs of both experienced and novice teachers.

Evaluation of the Mandated Program

Since the beginning of the foreign language mandate, we have employed two types of evaluation studies: analysis of students' test scores and program evaluation conducted by outside evaluators. We have developed a local assessment instrument to determine the elementary school pupils' level of French and Spanish mastery. The Baltimore Elementary Foreign Language Test has been used and refined since 1983. This test demonstrates that the elementary pupils in the pilot are achieving the course expectancies. Three levels of each test have been developed and used; each measures pupils' basic knowledge of elementary oral and aural language.

Local college and community personnel have been involved in conducting independent evaluations of our program. In the spring of 1986, evaluators visited schools to confer with staff and students about the foreign language program.

Conclusions

Our experiment can succeed. It has been and continues to be successful. Students are studying languages in the prescribed sequence. Positions have been staffed, with no small degree of effort. Materials have been deployed and redeployed; there are no grave shortages. Parents support the program. Initially parents asked for an expanded foreign language program. They voiced their request through various channels: principals, regional parent advisory councils, and the Board of School Commissioners. Our Office of Foreign Languages supervisory staff met with parent groups around the city as implementation progressed. The staff explained the curriculum, responded to concerns, and carefully considered suggestions. Indeed, there are parent groups who want more languages and more instruction in elementary schools. Many administrators now champion the cause of increased foreign language studies, going beyond the system's requirements for their schools. Increasingly, teachers of other disciplines are indicating to administrators, to the foreign language supervisory staff, and to the language teachers on the teams that such instruction reinforces skills across the curriculum. English language arts and social studies teachers are particularly aware of the positive carry-over effects of language study. Students appear to be accepting their newly required courses without unusual resistance. Indeed, judging from the number of schools featuring special Foreign Language Week programs, festivals, and displays, and the number of students involved, I would say that they are enjoying the new experience.

But we have learned several important lessons. The mandate — or any new program — can work only if the people involved in its implementation are involved at its inception. At the very beginning, it is necessary to get the best thinking of key players: principals, personnel and financial officers, and, most important, teachers. Contact with these members of the team must be maintained as the program is implemented. And the communication must be two-way. We all need to listen as well as to provide expertise, direction, and advice. In fact, perhaps our most critical contribution is sensitive listening.

We need to realize that our teachers are competent, that they are creative. They are a valuable resource in adapting old materials and in creating a new curriculum. They are carrying out the mandate; they should be the ones who help determine what they teach and how they teach it. We need to make use of our teachers in evaluating the program. They are the ones who see how it functions on a daily basis.

We need to know also that nothing worthwhile is accomplished cheaply. There is always a cost in dislocation of other programs and people with anything as wide in scope as the mandate. And, yes, there are additional costs. An expanded program requires books, more teachers, staff development, and new curriculum. But it is important to know that the expenditures are not catastrophic. The dislocations are generally temporary. And the benefits are substantial.

We need to understand that nothing is accomplished totally as planned, nor can significant change be accomplished overnight. Even after a mandate has been approved and publicized, there will be schools where the directive is not implemented right away, or correctly, or with conviction. There will be spot shortages of people and materials. There will be misinterpretation of directives. Implementation takes time, patience, and perseverance. It is necessary to maintain a constant monitoring effort. It is equally important to expect change. The staying power of the mandate has been bolstered by our ability to make adjustments and to fine-tune them. For example, at the start of this school year we made language an option in grade six and increased it to a daily program in grade eight. By doing so we terminated the alternate day scheduling.

A major instructional innovation such as the foreign language mandate is not hatched without breaking some shells. We needed conviction, commitment, and collaboration. Our doubters and detractors made us consider each aspect and resolve the foreseeable difficulties before they could injure the project. As a result, today in Baltimore, the street language of our youngest teenagers may be Latin, French, or Spanish.

One seventh grader told me: "When I was little, my parents always spelled when they didn't want me to know what they were saying. Now my sister and I speak French when we don't want anyone to understand." Who said that foreign language study isn't practical?

RICHARD C. WALLACE, JR., has been Superintendent of Schools in Pittsburgh (PA) since 1980 where full support from the Board of Education has enabled him to engineer a school-improvement program unparalleled in recent decades. His efforts incorporate a district-wide achievement monitoring program; intensive staff development, including the nationally acclaimed Schenley High School and Brookline Elementary Teacher Centers; and curriculum development in the areas of critical thinking and computer technology.

Upon graduation from Gorham (ME) State College, Mr. Wallace began his career as a teacher and principal in school districts in Maine. Between 1960 and 1966, while earning his master's and doctoral degrees from Boston College, he made the transition from classroom teacher to administrator. From 1968 to 1973, he was involved in the field of educational research. Following a year as a Postdoctoral Fellow in Educational Research at Stanford University, he served as Director of the Eastern Regional Institute for Education in Syracuse, and later was deputy director for program planning and evaluation at the Research and Development Center for Teacher Education at the University of Texas–Austin.

In his years in Pittsburgh, Mr. Wallace has demonstrated his talent as an educational leader by earning substantial corporate and foundation support for his new initiatives and by forging partnerships with the area's many universities and colleges. He is an adjunct professor in the University of Pittsburgh's Graduate School of Education, and a research associate for the University's Learning Research and Development Center for which he recently completed a paper entitled, "The Superintendent of Education."

MARY ELLEN KIRBY, as a parent volunteer, led the parent initiative to establish a strong sequence of foreign language studies in the magnet program in Pittsburgh. She formerly taught English at both Iowa State University and the University of Pittsburgh before becoming a public relations supervisor for a steel corporation.

In 1984 she was hired as a community relations consultant for the Pittsburgh Public Schools and was responsible for recruitment for the magnet programs. She is currently both a magnet recruiter and a community relations specialist for Pittsburgh.

THEKLA F. FALL is Associate Director of Foreign Language education in the Pittsburgh (PA) Public Schools, having taught German there since 1969 until assuming that position in 1982. She is responsible for the total design, implementation, evaluation, and maintenance of the foreign language and ESL programs for a total of 31 schools and 121 teachers.

Ms. Fall designed and implemented the instructional program for the International Studies Middle School Academy and the high school program to complete a 12-year span in Pittsburgh. She also expanded the International Studies program from 250 students to over 1,000 students and led the development of the International Baccalaureate program for French, German, and Spanish.

Richard C. Wallace, Jr., Mary Ellen Kirby,
and Thekla F. Fall

Commitment to Excellence: Community Collaboration in Pittsburgh

Introduction

Fourth-grade students solve multiplication and long division problems in Spanish. Students in the sixth, seventh, and eighth grades perform a short version of Humperdinck's *Hansel and Gretel* in German. High school juniors and seniors discuss theories of human nature according to Plato, Christianity, Freud, Lorenz, Marx, Sartre, and Skinner with philosophers from the Department of Philosophy and the Department of the History and Philosophy of Science of the University of Pittsburgh. The activities listed above illustrate how Pittsburgh Public Schools' students are reaping the rewards of successful collaboration among several key groups. Public school teachers and administrators are collaborating with parents, corporations, civic organizations, and university resources to establish foreign language learning and international status as a key component in the district's Excellence With Equity program.

Desegregation Tool

Realizing the importance of community collaboration, the Pittsburgh Board of Public Education encouraged parent participation in the educational process during the seventies when the court order to desegregate the schools weighed heavily on the district. Citizen advisory committees were formed to develop recommendations on many of the major issues relating to desegregation that faced the district. The dissolution of the neighborhood school concept, caused by the closing of 25 elementary schools in the 1980s, extensive redistricting, and mandatory busing, challenged the district to come up with an educational plan to prevent the wholesale defection of the white middle class to private and parochial schools.

The recommendation of one such advisory committee in 1979 was to introduce a foreign language magnet program, offering French, German, Italian, and Spanish in four city elementary schools. The Board of Education adopted the recommendation and the International Studies Program was initiated. Italian failed to attract enough applicants to open a class the same year that the other three language classes opened. After a late start, a change of location, and continued inability to attract black students, Italian was phased out, beginning in 1983. The French, German, and Spanish classes, however, have flourished. The initial 150 students enrolled in the first and second grades in 1979 have increased to more than 1,000 students enrolled in 1986 in grades one through five. The program has expanded in the three original elementary schools and has been replicated in two additional elementary schools, with one more school scheduled to open first- and second-grade Spanish magnet classes in 1987. To date, the program is racially balanced in all schools and has contributed, along with many other magnet programs such as the traditional and classical academies, toward the successful desegregation of the Pittsburgh Public Schools.

Parent Recruiters

From the onset, parents and community leaders have been active participants in the planning and implementation of the magnet, which emphasizes foreign language and international studies. Parent confidence in the program designed to lead young children to proficiency in French, German, or Spanish, in fact, preceded a written curriculum and the hiring of teachers to present such a curriculum.

During the first few years of the program, parents were pleased with the excellent progress their children were making not only in the foreign language but in other academic subjects as well. These parents, who enjoyed all the benefits of voluntary integration as well as an excellent foreign language program, recruited other parents to the program with missionary zeal. Parental recruitment still remains as one of the hallmarks of the successful magnet programs.

Parents were anxious for their children to have the opportunity to capitalize on their elementary school success and wanted to be sure that the promised middle school and high school expansion of the program became a reality. Parents presented their recommendations and expectations to the Board of Education and the administration, founding their request for a magnet middle school on the success and growing popularity of the elementary program. The Board responded by agreeing to open Dilworth School as the International Studies Academy, provided there were enough students interested at all three grade levels to justify opening a new magnet middle school.

The Foreign Language Magnet Advisory Committee was chaired by a parent dedicated to excellence in public education and willing to work wholeheartedly on behalf of the international studies program. The parents on this committee responded to the Board's charge by composing, printing, and direct mailing to selected target students a brochure extolling the advantages of an international studies middle school. Although only 40 students from the foreign language magnet fifth-grade classes were committed to continue into the sixth grade, parents recruited enough additional applicants to net a total of 180 sixth-, seventh-, and eighth-grade students to open the new International Studies Academy in 1983. Thirty-four students were on a waiting list for the sixth grade. In three years, the Dilworth International Studies Academy has been forced to move to Frick School, a larger facility that can accommodate the anticipated influx of 150 to 200 sixth-grade students each year.

The surprising groundswell of parental support forced the district to reevaluate this magnet program beyond its function as a desegregation tool. The decline in heavy industry and the emergence of Pittsburgh as a major international trade center, coupled with the various commission reports that heralded "global awareness" and promoted foreign language learning, spearheaded the thrust toward international education. Thus, the original goal of foreign language learning has evolved in the last three years into the larger context of an international studies program that now encompasses all subject areas: English, mathematics, science, social studies, the arts, and physical education, as well as foreign language.

District planning for a secondary school international studies program coincided with planning for the middle school. Ideally, the high school program could have been opened sequentially in order to capitalize on the strong body of students (and their parents) who had been enrolled in the program from the beginning. The Board of Education had agreed to a plan to desegregate voluntarily Schenley High School in 1982, building on four magnet programs, to achieve that goal. A four-year international studies program that would include the widely acclaimed International Baccalaureate in grades 11 and 12 was designed to help achieve the goal of racial balance in the school.

With a strong academic emphasis on international and interdisciplinary curriculum in mind, program planning began in 1982 with parent groups, district staff, and personnel from the University Center for International Studies (UCIS) at the University of Pittsburgh. The high school program was implemented in 1983, the same year that the International Studies Middle School was opened. Sixteen students enrolled in the first ninth-grade class.

The Pennsylvania Human Relations Commission's acceptance of the district's desegregation plan in 1982 was dependent, in large part, on the voluntary desegregation of Schenley High School. Desegregation of Schenley High School was dependent on the attraction of white students primarily to the International Studies and International Baccalaureate magnet. Considering the great demand generated for the elementary and middle school components of the program, the district realized the need for organized recruitment and the value of parents as recruiters.

With funding from the Frick Educational Commission, the district hired two parent advocates to market the international studies magnet program and the school to other parents and to recruit students. White student enrollment in the magnet program grade nine has increased from four in 1983 to approximately 50 in 1986. The public perception of the school, fostered by parents whose children have had positive experiences there, has improved dramatically over the past four years.

Evaluation

Parent confidence in the program has not been misplaced. Evaluation reports of the elementary foreign language program during the first two years compared the mathematics and reading achievement of the students enrolled in the foreign language magnets with their grade level peers nationally, districtwide, and in their host schools. In both years, foreign language magnet students at all grade levels (one, two, three) either equalled or out-performed their counterparts in reading and mathematics. Their teachers' high evaluations of their progress were confirmed by the students' standardized test scores in reading and mathematics, initially on the Metropolitan Achievement Test and in all subsequent years on the California Achievement Test (CAT).

In the three original host schools, where the foreign language magnet enrollment now constitutes 50 to 80 percent of total enrollment, achievement scores have been consistently high, especially in the language portion of the CAT. Eighty-seven to 91 percent of the students in the three schools scored at or above the national norm in

1985, with 66 to 70 percent scoring in the top quarter nationally in language, and only one to four percent in the bottom quarter.

The Dilworth International Studies Academy outscored all other middle schools in the district on the 1985 CAT in language, with 93 percent of the 260 students tested scoring at or above the national norm, 71 percent in the top quarter and none in the bottom quarter.

Similarly, scores have been high in reading and mathematics on the CAT. In reading 81 percent of the pupils scored above the norm on the 1985 CAT in elementary schools, and 83 percent scored above the norm in middle school (more than half scoring in the top quarter nationally); in mathematics 82 to 88 percent scored above the norm in elementary, and 91 percent scored above the norm in middle school (54 to 64 percent scoring in the top quarter).

Student achievement in the foreign language initially was less definitively assessed. From the beginning, two essential areas of concern were the basis on which the program would be structured and how the program and student progress would be evaluated. For the first three years of the foreign language program, teachers' evaluations were based on mutually agreed upon objectives. These informal indices were the only data gathered on student progress.

After much consideration, a solution to both the problem of structure and evaluation was found in the American Council on the Teaching of Foreign Languages and Educational Testing Service (ACTFL/ETS) Proficiency Standards. The first proficiency interviews with the fifth-grade German, Spanish, and French magnet students were conducted in the spring of 1984.[1]

The results were encouraging. The students were judged to be at about the same level of speaking proficiency as high school students who had studied a foreign language for two years. The younger children, however, spoke with a near native pronunciation and were much less inhibited in conversation than their high school counterparts.

In 1985, and again in 1986, fifth-grade students from the elementary foreign language magnet schools were interviewed by local university personnel, in accordance with ACTFL/ETS Oral Proficiency Standards.[2] These university professors have taken a personal interest in the program and have served on the various advisory committees. They have volunteered their time in addition to serving in an official consultant capacity.

Thus, oral proficiency testing has become another important area of collaboration. Used primarily as a formative evaluation, the ratings and individual student profiles provide valuable information to program planners. According to current plans there will be additional testing in grades eight and twelve to monitor the effectiveness of the program as well as to document individual student progress through the 12-year sequence. The professors have also offered to interview faculty members on a confidential basis. The collaboration will expand over the next year to include a revision of the curriculum based on the proficiency standards and inservice workshops that focus on teaching for proficiency.

Although students from the original elementary foreign language magnet classes are enrolled in the ninth grade of the international studies magnet at Schenley High School for the first time in 1986, high academic achievement in all subjects has also been the norm for the high school participants in the program since 1983. Three of the original ninth-grade students have maintained a perfect 4.0 grade average during their first three years of high school. Two of the three also participated in a six-week foreign student exchange trip to Canada during their sophomore year and are now strong candidates for the International Baccalaureate Diploma.

Collaboration — Joint Ownership

The opportunity for teachers, parents, and university advisers to collaborate in the development of a new program has provided a dynamic sense of ownership. Participants take pride in the program they have helped to create and are zealous in their efforts to promote, expand, and improve it. All are willing to "go the extra mile" to insure that the program achieves its goals. Students are affected by the contagious enthusiasm and high expectations of their teachers and parents and are inspired to put forth their very best effort.

To stay abreast of the higher expectations and achievement levels, the district has intensified staff inservice training. A Foreign Language Advisory Committee, an extension of one of the task forces of the 1984 Pittsburgh Citizens Committee on Excellence in Education, has been meeting regularly to address the following issues related to international studies and foreign languages: staff development, student testing, standardization and expansion of the curriculum in the standard middle schools, articulation from high school to the college and university level, the introduction of foreign language experiences in the standard elementary school curriculum. The committee is comprised of teachers, parents, central administrative staff, and personnel from three local universities and the community college. The district and the institutions of higher learning have benefited mutually from the exchange of information and ideas emanating from this committee.

Indiana University of Pennsylvania, for example, recently was awarded a federal grant to pilot a program to enable elementary education majors to earn both an elementary foreign language teaching certificate and an elementary teaching certificate simultaneously. The dean who designed the program is optimistic about the prospects of employment for her dual certification graduates. The district, too, is encouraged by the potential pool of qualified teachers from which to recruit and hire.

Local university and community college faculty are providing support services to the school district, including inservice speakers, student tutors, and specialty courses for maintenance and diversification of foreign language skills for foreign language teachers. Plans have been developed to facilitate college placement and to award college credit for the successful completion of advanced level high school courses. The university teachers are also preparing to receive high school graduates whose foreign language proficiency exceeds that of the average incoming freshman.

Co-Teaching

The University of Pittsburgh Center for International Studies is a major partner with the Schenley High School International Studies and International Baccalaureate magnet; however, the involvement of the liberal arts faculty and the School of Education is equally important. High school teachers and university professors have worked together to develop a unique, academically challenging curriculum for the special courses in the magnet program. Professors who are distinguished scholars in their field and can also relate well to high school students are sharing teaching responsibilities in the classrooms of their high school colleagues. The response to the first classroom collaborations has been positive from the high school teachers, the professors, and the students.

An interesting sideline is that the University of Pittsburgh professor of history who collaborated in the writing and teaching of the International Baccalaureate History of the Americas course is also the father of a second-grade student in the German international studies magnet. The high school American history teacher with whom the professor collaborates is the father of a fourth-grade student in the Spanish international studies magnet. This "overlap" was discovered after the collaborative teaching arrangement had been negotiated. Both have also become active members of the International Studies Advisory Committee.

Ronald Butera, the Schenley High School teacher, endorses the collaboration, commenting, "I feel that Dr. Andrews' presence in the classroom greatly enhanced the course curriculum without any interference with the flow of the prepared outline. Professor Andrews and I related on a personal and collegial level that enabled him to teach and plan with me in a welcomed atmosphere of professionalism."

Equally successful has been the collaboration of internationally distinguished philosopher/scholars in the Theory of Knowledge course, required for International Baccalaureate Diploma candidates at Schenley High School. Dr. Nuel Belnap, who is the Alan Ross Anderson Distinguished Professor of Philosophy, Professor of Sociology, and Professor of the History and Philosophy of Science, University of Pittsburgh, has been the coordinating consultant for both the first-year and the second-year course of the Theory of Knowledge. The professors made very engaging presentations of highly complex concepts at a level both interesting and comprehensible to the high school students.

A concerted effort to capitalize on these initial, highly successful collaborations was made in March, 1985, during a one and one-half day international studies workshop. The district's curriculum directors and the Schenley High School international studies teachers in the disciplines of English, mathematics, foreign language (French, German, Spanish), social studies, and science (biology, chemistry, physics) worked with their counterparts from the university. Faculty members from the University of Pittsburgh School of Arts and Sciences and the Center for International Studies, Duquesne University, Carnegie-Mellon University and Chatham College joined with the district's personnel to plan courses of study. Exciting outlines for 12th-grade courses, uniquely international and interdisciplinary, were developed. A strong feeling of joint ownership and a bond of commitment to the program were cultivated equally among the university faculty and high school teachers.

The 12th-grade International Studies Seminar, being introduced this year, will focus on four major topics of global significance: media perceptions, economics, migration, and human rights. Collaborating with the Schenley High School teachers are the University Center for International Studies associate directors of Russian and East European Studies, Latin American Studies and History, and Western European Studies, and an associate professor of law in the University of Pittsburgh Law School. The university faculty presentations will be an integral part of the overall curriculum and will occur an average of once a week during each of four six-week concentrations.

This collaboratively planned, consistently implemented program which is developing at Schenley High School is a significant step up from the occasional enrichment or supplemental lecture series by visiting scholars attached to the university field service; however, this lecture service will also continue. Also significant is the participation of university faculty in the international studies magnet classes as well as the International Baccalaureate Program and the Advanced Placement Program in grades 11 and 12.

The Pennsylvania Governor's School for International Studies, a prestigious summer scholarship program for academically talented high school sophomores and juniors, has been permanently assigned to the University of Pittsburgh. The recently appointed Director of the Governor's School has been the University Center for International Studies liaison working with the middle and high school international studies programs. A day-long symposium on world hunger, for example, was coordinated at the International Studies Academy; and a cross-cultural experience for high school and middle school teachers was conducted with assistance from the Director of the Governor's School. The physical proximity of the Frick International Studies Academy and Schenley High School to the university facilities — all within easy walking distance — and the close working relationship between district and university personnel provide mutually advantageous opportunities for collaboration. Because of this collaboration, Pittsburgh can truly say that it is well on its way to establishing a sequential foreign language and international studies program that starts in first grade and continues through college and post-graduate studies.

Parent/Teacher Support

One of the strongest endorsements of the international studies magnet is the number of public and private school teachers who have enrolled their own children in the program. In Pittsburgh, where first-come, first-served has been the established method of enrollment in magnet schools, parents have been lining up as early as 68 hours ahead of the opening hour of registration for the elementary program. For example, three teachers in the Spanish program have stood alongside other hopeful parents, waiting to submit applications for their children. The impact of this commitment has been phenomenal. Teachers, administrators, and central staff have children, grandchildren, nephews and nieces enrolling at all three entry levels of the program. Such heavy involvement helps increase the probability of sustained commitment to the program and stimulates excellence at all grade levels.

The close collaboration of parent/teacher, parent/community support is also evident in such organizations as the Allegheny Conference on Community Development. The 43-year-old Allegheny Conference is made up of approximately 30 major corporations in Pittsburgh and has taken an active role in the support of public education. The Assistant Executive Director of the Conference has had two children enrolled in the international studies magnet program from the year it began. The current administrator of the Conference Education Program is also a parent of two children enrolled in the Spanish elementary program. Such parents, working together and in close harmony with district professionals, have maintained a high level of support and expectation, both for an enriched curriculum and for sustained excellence in teaching.

Collaboration between the schools and the corporate/civic community is best illustrated, perhaps, by the Allegheny Conference Education Fund. Over the past eight years, several mini-grants have been awarded to teachers in the international studies magnet program. A second-grade teacher used $200, for example, to purchase the necessary cooking utensils and food for her children to prepare several Spanish, Mexican, or South American dishes. The children learned the names, colors, and flavors of each food item, and the measurements, terms for preparation, and cultural significance of six different dishes. At the end of the year they concluded this activity with a feast.

Bilingual signs have been placed throughout the schools where the program is housed, and 50 students in grades six and seven with support from Conference grants have exchanged letters, photographs, and artwork with their counterparts in Loma Bonita School in a remote village in Panama. The mother of one of the academy students is an anthropologist who has been studying the people of Loma Bonita, living with them in the summers for the past several years and sharing her experiences with her son's Spanish magnet class annually.

Impact on the District

The publicity generated by the popular international studies magnet program has awakened the general public to the need and subsequent demand for an improved foreign language curriculum in the non-magnet schools. The impact of the magnet programs on the district has led to a revitalization of the standard foreign language curriculum and a reorganization of the administration of the program. Within the last four years, an associate director of foreign language and a foreign language teacher on special assignment have been appointed to supervise the expanding foreign language program throughout the district.

The standard middle school program in foreign language has been completely reorganized and standardized. A new introductory Latin-based language course (The Phenomenon of Language) was implemented in the 1985–86 school year for all sixth-grade students. Seventh-grade students can now elect to study a modern foreign language in a two-year sequence in middle school and continue with the same language throughout four years of high school. The opportunity for advanced study to gain functional fluency in a second language is thus available to all students in the district in addition to those in the international studies magnet program.

The demand for the elementary international studies magnet program, however, continues to exceed the number of available spaces. Finding high quality teachers with elementary school certification who are fluent in a second language continues to be a major obstacle to expansion. This has been particularly true of the German magnet program. The middle school goal of offering at least one academic subject in the foreign language has been frustrated, in part, by the scarcity of teachers who are certified in a foreign language as well as mathematics, science, or other disciplines, and in part by the necessity to group the students according to their academic levels rather than their target language. The increasing number of advanced students coming to the Frick International Studies Academy, should permit the scheduling of some immersion reinforcement classes. For example, mathematics, social studies, or science could be offered in German, French, or Spanish in the coming years.

Other plans for reinforcement and foreign language maintenance include a one-week immersion camp for students in grades nine and ten on the Chatham College campus during August 1987. These students will have an opportunity to get to know one another in an informal recreational setting, thus bridging the gap between middle school and high school, while at the same time sharpening their foreign language skills and raising their global awareness.

In a secluded sylvan setting at Chatham College, within the city limits, the students will share a simulated living experience in a French, German, or Spanish speaking community, where no English is spoken, no American currency is permitted, and no American food will be available. Senior high school students in the international studies program, some of whom have attended the Concordia College summer immersion camp in Moorhead, Minnesota, and have traveled abroad during their summers, will collaborate with teachers on the daily plans for the camp and will serve as junior counselors. The Director of the Governor's School will assist in the identification and screening of counselors, many of whom are expected to have had experience as counselors at the Governor's School for International Studies on the University of Pittsburgh campus.

Mutual Commitment

Finally, then, collaboration is working effectively in Pittsburgh because all parties are committed to the pursuit of excellence in the public schools. Parents, university faculty, and community organizations are not being called upon to remedy a desperate situation. Rather, responsibility for planning, developing, and implementing effective educational programs is shared among the participants. Parents who have a vested interest in a particular program or school have the opportunity to make responsible recommendations, reflecting their expectations of the district and expressing their willingness to do their share of the work to help the district meet those expectations. The district has responded with sensitivity and respect to thoughtful parent involvement.

High school teachers who are participating in co-teaching arrangements with university faculty have had nothing foisted upon them and are in no way displaced or diminished in the classroom. They have final selection of recommended university specialists to assure compatibility, and the partnership is developed under their direction, largely of their own design. These classroom collaborations provide the opportunity for professional development and increased scholarship for high school teachers.

The university professors have responded very positively to the overtures of the district. Starting global education as early as possible is a high priority for them. There are also some very practical as well as philosophical advantages for those scholars who are involved in the research and writing of high school textbooks. They have the opportunity to field test their materials and obtain immediate reactions from high school teachers and students.

The corporate/civic community has enjoyed an excellent return on its investment in the public schools. In Rand McNally's rating of Pittsburgh as the nation's most livable city, public education received the highest score among all of the criteria used to judge livability.

The Pittsburgh Board of Education has included community and parental involvement in its list of 1986 priorities. As further evidence of the commitment to collaboration, the district has begun negotiations to facilitate the university/district teaching partnerships by hiring a liaison officer who will be employed jointly by the district and the University of Pittsburgh.

Pittsburgh is looking forward to a longstanding, continuing collaborative relationship with all its school partnerships. Through these collaborative efforts the district has made significant strides in improving the quality of education for the youth of the city.

Notes

1 June Phillips, Professor of Foreign Languages and Literatures and Associate Dean of the College of Humanities at Indiana University of Pennsylvania, and Judith Liskin-Gasparro, senior examiner for Educational Testing Service, volunteered to conduct the first proficiency interviews with fifth-grade students in 1984.

2 Benjamin Hicks, Beverly Harris-Schenz, and Rosario Caminero are all from the Foreign Language Departments of the University of Pittsburgh.

MADELINE EHRLICH is the founder and President of Advocates for Language Learning, an organization promoting and supporting bilingualism in education. She lives in Culver City, California, with her husband Paul and their three children who are all enrolled in Spanish immersion classes in their local public school. By profession, she is a registered nurse currently working part time.

Mrs. Ehrlich grew up on the East Coast, raised by parents whose first language was French. Though her parents later learned English in school, both were fluent in their first language. In fact, her mother preferred speaking French and wanted to speak that language to her children. However, Mrs. Ehrlich's father felt that being "American" meant speaking only English and decided to eliminate French conversation from their home.

As an adult, Mrs. Ehrlich has had the opportunity to live in three large U.S. cities and to see firsthand that speaking a second language is not only useful but at times essential. As a practicing nurse caring for patients who could not speak English, she realized that nursing skills alone were inadequate.

Because her own experiences taught her so much about language learning and about the limitations of speaking a single language, she has become a passionate promoter of second language education for children and believes that a quality education for every child should include the opportunity to become bilingual.

Madeline Ehrlich

Parents:
The Child's Most Important Teachers

Introduction

Who laughed and smiled and exclaimed as Baby spoke his first "Mama" and "Dada" sounds? His parents, of course! And they taught him that those sounds had special meaning as words. Every time he said a word, he got the same positive encouragement from his family. That powerful force "taught" him his primary language almost from the day he was born.

Parents teach their children all the time in many subtle ways; they use a natural approach and scarcely realize the complexity of what they are doing. By the time children enter kindergarten, their feelings about themselves and how they perceive the world are already molded into their characters. Even though these children are increasingly exposed to many different experiences and points of view, they continue to be primarily influenced by their parents throughout their early years in the areas of attitudes, values, and self esteem. This influence, whether positive or negative, is often *the* deciding factor in how children perceive other peoples, cultures, and languages.

Sharing information with parents and teachers working together to build effective second language programs is the purpose of this paper. It is written from the perspective of an enthusiastic, involved parent who has accepted the teacher's challenge to contribute time and effort to improve the second language program. Most of what I have written comes from my personal experiences in raising my own children bilingually, hosting many exchange students from around the world as they acquired and mastered the English language, and discussing the many facets of second language education with fellow parents and many dedicated educators. I have also included some suggestions from my many correspondents and from reading about language programs all over the world. Most of my suggestions are about how parents can become valuable assets to their children's second language program. I will also focus on how teachers can harness this positive parental support and build stronger world language programs.

Background

During the late 1950s when world interest in science was very high because of the space race between the United States and the Soviet Union, educators critically examined the curricula in both countries and decided that American schools did not emphasize science and mathematics enough. They also identified a deficit in world language study. But initial enthusiasm arose quickly and died just as fast. Little attempt was made to enlist public support for the new curricula; once the newness of the space program had subsided and other issues were more prominent in the press, whatever momentum the movement had was gone. Perhaps this was even more critical in the case of languages because popular opinion has looked upon such study as a frill rather than a necessity.

Now in the 1980s, we again see a resurgence of interest in the area of second language studies. This time it comes not only from the educators but from the community as well. Television has exposed many of us to other cultures. Low cost travel opportunities have given some of us personal experiences from many lands. Parents are becoming more aware of the real need to raise bilingual children in our world and have begun to insist upon better language programs in our schools. And although it is coming slowly, research data on the positive effects of second language learning are finally getting to the consumer. The key to sustaining this new emphasis on world languages in our schools will be the support of parents and educators working together.

Because the attitudes surrounding second language learning are so critical to its success, avoiding any negative connotations is most important. The Foreign Language Office of the Minnesota Department of Education has taken a decisive step in a positive direction by renaming their Department of Foreign Language Studies as the Department of World Language Studies. The word "foreign" often provokes feelings of anxiety about aliens as a threat to the American way of life whereas the term "world" suggests feelings of brotherhood and global unity. If a simple change in terminology will help Americans see that learning a second language is a way to build bridges to fellow human beings, then we who are in a position to influence that change should make the effort without delay.

Advocates for Language Learning (ALL)

Some time after my husband and I made the decision to enroll our oldest child in a language immersion program in our school district, I realized that fellow parents had been instrumental in convincing us of the value of second language immersion for our child. Their excitement about the program and their conviction that early second language education is important to the child and to the world he lives in was what had influenced our thinking. And we, in turn, caught their enthusiasm and have shared it with many more people. But I came to realize that many parents who share similar ideas about world language education for their children feel isolated because we participate in an experience which is not yet widely understood and accepted within the community. At the same time the immersion program teachers, who are very few in number and frequently come to our school from many different areas of the city, feel alone in their classroom efforts. Various professional organizations exist for secondary level world language teachers and for bilingual teachers whose focus is helping minority students learn English. But teachers in immersion and other elementary world language programs are in a separate category which lacks that organized support. There was a definite need for a cohesive group to share information and provide support to one another.

For these reasons and because I began to envision an educational environment where every child would have the opportunity to learn a second language as a part of the regular school program, I founded Advocates for Language Learning in December 1983. The original members were a small group of parents and educators from our own school district in Culver City, CA. I recall that first night when a handful of us got together in my home to discuss forming a support organization. We discussed the scope of our effort—should it be a parent booster club for our school only? No; if we truly wanted to enrich the educational opportunities for all children, we would need grass roots support from all over the country. We could start in our own neighborhood, but sharing ideas and experiences with other parents and educators was the way to our goal. We must act locally and think globally. Someone asked whether the word "advocate" was too strong for a support group of parents and teachers. Again, no; the day has come when we need to be "advocates" for the study of world languages. We need the strength of people truly committed to building bridges to other nations and cultures in our world.

ALL is an association of parents, teachers, and other individuals interested in promoting and enhancing the study of second languages for children. It acts as an information sharing resource on educational opportunities in second language acquisition for parents, educators, government bodies, and the general public. Its success depends on the combined efforts and involvement of each and every person who feels that bilingualism is important. ALL's goals include ensuring that every child has the opportunity to acquire knowledge of a second language and culture; promoting the most effective kinds of second language programs; and establishing effective communication among parents, educators, and government authorities who are responsible for providing language learning opportunities.

Since those early days, ALL has quickly moved from a small community group to a national organization with chapters in several U.S. cities. What makes ALL unique is that a strong parent component works with educational providers toward a mutual goal—the availability of quality world language programs in our schools. Local chapters can identify community needs and resources. The national organization can address broader issues such as the education of our legislators on the value of using world languages to preserve our multicultural American heritage and to enhance the opportunities for global peace.

Chapters have sponsored student recruitment into new and existing elementary school language programs. Scholarship programs to enable a student to continue his education beyond the secondary school level have been established. Our own local chapter has set up an exchange program between our school and an elementary school in Guadalajara, Mexico. Fifth- and sixth-grade students from both countries can spend a month with a host family experiencing the language and culture firsthand. In fact, our local community support was so enthusiastic that Mexican students were housed with several local families who did not have children in the second language program.

Members of ALL have sponsored three international conferences since the organization was founded. Speakers and conferees from across the U.S., Canada, and Europe met to exchange ideas and discuss issues and common goals for educators and parents. The 1986 conference was hosted by the Milwaukee chapter in that city; the 1987 conference will be held on the East Coast. California chapters have been especially successful in developing a positive working relationship with the state department of education, and members have testified before legislative committees on behalf of bilingual education.

Educating the Parents

Because ALL is an organization of individuals, many of whom are parents, let me begin with a discussion of how teachers can approach and involve parents in the second language education process.

Is it possible for parents to be actively involved with and supportive of a second language program when they can neither understand nor speak that language? The answer is a definite *yes*! But the key to capturing and harnessing parental enthusiasm is to set realistic expectations at the beginning. The more knowledge parents have about the language program — its value, its perspective, its goals and objectives — the more supportive they can be. Giving the parents a clear picture of what their children will be learning, how they will be learning it, and the level of linguistic competence they will have when they complete the program, will help to avoid misunderstandings later when the children are enrolled in the language program.

Perhaps it is important to point out here that the reasons why children study a second language can be very different depending on the age of the child. Usually parents make the decision to enroll their elementary school children in a second language program because of their own beliefs about the value of studying a second language. Often, however, secondary school students take language courses because of high school graduation or college admissions requirements rather than because of their interest in knowing a second language. While this does not mean that parents of younger students are always more supportive and involved than others, they may have much higher expectations for their children because they initiated the effort to give their children this opportunity.

Many parents of school age children have studied another language themselves at some time, usually in high school or college. Often the teaching methods and course goals were totally unlike those of second language programs today. Drilling verb tenses and translating newspaper articles is very different from building practical vocabulary with everyday activities and children's stories. Even though a child may be progressing well in a program which uses a natural approach, his parent may be concerned that the child is not receiving enough emphasis on grammar. One example is that of a family with two children enrolled in an elementary school immersion program. Initially, the parents were led to believe that their children would be able to use the second language with the skill of native speakers by the end of sixth grade. Research published after their children had begun the program showed that earlier predictions were overly optimistic in that area and that immersion students did not have identical skills to those of native speakers. This information was never given to parents of children in the language program. Even though their oldest child had achieved a high level of proficiency by the time he finished elementary school, he was not a carbon copy of a native speaker. The parents felt that they had been misled and were much less supportive of the program thereafter.

How can families possibly be effective supporters of a program about which they are ignorant? I cannot emphasize enough how important it is for teachers and administrators to maintain an ongoing dialogue with the parents. Regular meetings (in the evening or on Saturday so working parents are included) are excellent opportunities for teachers to present the program, discuss goals and current methodology, explain how parents can become involved, and point out problems needing the attention of the group.

Occasional meetings can be structured as parent workshops or can feature invited guests with special areas of expertise. Parents of prospective students could see firsthand how the language program is presented and supported. Weekly newsletters with similar information can supplement the meetings and present timely reminders of upcoming events in which children will participate. Recruit parents as valuable allies and make sure that they are aware and informed of their child's language program. In addition, once a few of the parents have become knowledgeable about the program and its goals, they can be of great help in spreading the information to other parents and to the community.

Following are discussions of three areas where parents can be effectively involved in supporting and furthering their children's second language education.

Parents at Home

The fundamental relationship between parents and their children is centered in the home. The family unit is the source of love, security, values, attitudes, and ideas. Active support of the child's schoolwork as well as not-so-obvious guidance and encouragement can make an enormous difference in the ability of the child to learn a new language. Parents can create an environment which will foster positive attitudes toward second language study.

In their regular meetings and newsletters to parents, teachers can suggest many of the following activities and ideas for the parents to use in the family setting to encourage the child's efforts. One simple, inexpensive way parents can help a youngster build vocabulary is by making signs to put on household objects. The child should be actively involved in selecting not only what to label, but what kind of paper, what color of ink, what size to make the sign, and how to safely attach the signs to various kinds of material. A similar activity is to cut out pictures from magazines and newspapers and make a poster or booklet with the correct names next to the objects.

Another way parents can expose their children to their new language is through music. Singing along with simple songs or dancing to lively instrumental music is especially fun for young children and it's easy for other members of the family to participate (by clapping, for example) even though they may not know the words themselves. Libraries, children's bookstores, and curriculum materials outlets are places to find songbooks and records with music from all over the world. Storybook/tape combinations are available for smaller children. Often if more than one child in the family is studying the same language or if the parents have skills in the second language, story hour can be conducted in that language. Several board games such as picture bingo, Scrabble, Monopoly, and Clue are available in world languages. Many parents may not be aware of the variety of resources available within the community or through mail-order sources and would welcome suggestions from the teacher. Of course parents can become resources for one another as well by sharing what they have found valuable.

Parents can also greatly enhance their children's learning and understanding of a second language by encouraging them to read for pleasure in that language. It is important to start when the child is very young to develop the habit of reading in the second language; I have found that once children reach the age of ten or older, they are not as easily enticed to select books in the target language. Initial parental efforts to encourage recreational reading in the world language will involve supervision and guidance and will require patience as well. A special effort will be needed to have suitable material available when children express interest. Libraries in larger metropolitan areas may have children's literature available in several languages. For those who do not have sufficient resources in their areas as well as parents who wish to build a home library, I have included publishers and mail-order sources at the end of this Report.

Many families are enthusiastic about participating in community events held in ethnic neighborhoods where their child's second language is spoken. Local festivals featuring entertainment and special foods are often held at community centers and churches, sometimes with very little publicity outside their own small groups. Often the food is quite inexpensive and the entertainment is free. Teachers can make sure that parents are aware of these possibilities and can encourage them to call sponsoring organizations and get on their mailing lists. (It might also be useful for the teacher to get on the mailing lists in order to make suggestions to the class or the parents.) Some cities have a Bureau of Cultural Affairs which maintains a calendar of events; the Chamber of Commerce may also have information; a large university is likely to sponsor cultural events or have student groups which participate; and ethnic societies in many cities often have small offices which coordinate community activities. One activity for a group of interested parents at the beginning of the year might be to make the contacts suggested above and to develop a calendar of community events for the students to take home. Sending home information and encouraging the parents to join together and attend as a group can also have the side benefit of encouraging a cohesive class and a functioning parent support group. In addition, many ethnic restaurants offer meals at reasonable prices and provide entertainment during selected times. Seeing their parents enjoying activities outside of their usual everyday experience sends a profound message to the children about the value of people from other backgrounds and cultures.

Families who are more adventuresome may appreciate suggestions on preparing simple or more elaborate recipes from countries where their child's new language is spoken. If they live in cities where a large enough ethnic population is centered, attending family films at the theatre followed by a meal at a restaurant where the language is used could be a special outing. By all means, the child should be encouraged to speak the new language any time the opportunity is available such as in purchasing theatre tickets or ordering a meal. One note of caution, parents must use sensitivity here and not push a child who would prefer to be an observer rather than an active participant.

Older children who have acquired a high level of proficiency in a language used by a group within the community may be encouraged to utilize their skills in several ways. Reading storybooks at a day care center or pediatric ward in the hospital is often easy to arrange and particularly appreciated by adults who have many responsibilities other than providing individual attention to one or two children. Elderly people at a community center or **senior** housing project might welcome teenagers to read aloud, write letters, or simply sit and talk.

Sponsoring an exchange student who speaks the second language is another alternative which is often overlooked. Many programs will pay for the student's room and board; it isn't even essential that there be a private bedroom. Children can learn a great deal about another language and culture from other children. Although the visiting student will certainly want to absorb the American culture too, often this student will be very sympathetic to youngsters in the household who are learning that student's language and will help them practice. Over the past five years my own family has hosted 27 different students from all over the world. It has been very interesting and lots of fun; my son could write a book about all of the roommates he has had!

For those families who live close to our international borders or who have the opportunity to travel abroad, the excitement of a trip to another country is wonderful motivation to learn and use a second language. An awareness that people all over the world often think and feel in similar ways is much easier to develop when the child can see and hear it firsthand. If such a trip is a possibility, the teacher can work with the parents ahead of time to plan a few activities which will strengthen the language experience. Perhaps attending a children's theatre or visiting a museum with special interest for youngsters would be fun for everyone in the family. An additional suggestion is to plan shopping expeditions with an eye for purchasing games, puzzles, books, and other treasures which can become part of the learning experience once the family has returned home.

If one or both parents speak the world language studied by their children, they should make the effort to use it in the home. Perhaps the family will want to use the primary language as well as setting aside certain rooms or activities or times when the second language will be spoken. It is not unusual for children to respond to a question or comment in one language with their primary language. This might be because they are somewhat inhibited about using the new language in front of friends or it could simply be a matter of habit. I have devised games and small rewards for my own children to make using the target language more fun for them.

One point bears repeating here. No matter what parents do to support their children in learning a second language, the most effective encouragement is their own attitude. By expressing their feelings about how useful a world language can be when traveling, looking for a job, or just living on the planet, parents are sending a clear positive message of support. And finally, praise, praise, and more praise for their children's efforts will definitely pay off.

Parents at School

The primary influence in the classroom is clearly the teacher, but here, too, the parents can provide valuable assistance. It is important to realize that this may involve a change in the traditional role of the parents, and teachers must actively encourage the participation of parents. While a number of parents will come to school and volunteer on their own initiative, many others will wait to be invited. Through the ongoing parent meetings and newsletters, teachers can invite them to join in. A survey might be used to locate parents with skills to contribute. It is particularly important that the teacher specify ways volunteers can assist and how much time will be involved. Make sure that prospective volunteers understand that the teacher will oversee activities and give parents direction on what to do.

Because new ideas take time to become real-life actions, there are sure to be times when teachers feel that they are working against overwhelming odds which will never produce any benefit. But parents, too, are struggling with their own past experiences. Many have been discouraged from venturing into the teacher's territory or have been actively involved on school planning committees only to discover that their ideas and suggestions have been regarded as token participation by the school administration.

Overcoming such attitudes on both sides will take time, but it can definitely be done and is well worth the effort! Often parents who themselves do not speak the language being taught in the classroom or who feel that their skills are rusty are hesitant to volunteer to help with the program. However, there are many ways in which parents can help the teacher make the most of time with the students.

Arranging bulletin boards according to a teacher's sketch does not require second language skills and can be especially valuable in providing a changing atmosphere in the classroom. Performing clerical jobs which frees the teacher to spend more time with the students is also very welcome. Locating and contacting guest speakers or tracking down and obtaining unusual materials to be used in special projects often requires time and the persistence to follow up leads with phone calls. Even if the sources are businesses in the ethnic community, they are usually quite experienced in dealing with buyers who do not speak their language. Often parents can also help by supervising craft projects while the teacher spends time with another group or in another activity.

For those parents who have a little language experience, tasks such as correcting papers and preparing handout materials are possibilities. Frequently the teacher spends time on repetitious tasks which could be handled by someone with less training. Those who may have traveled abroad can bring pictures, slides, books, and gift items to share with the students. Their children in the class can help to prepare a script and can translate the presentation into the classroom language, or they can present jointly with the parent.

Of course, parents who do have proficiency in the language their children are studying can work with groups of students or individuals in the same way that other volunteers often assist in regular classrooms taught in the primary language. They can take responsibility for special projects with groups of students or lead the class in activities suggested by their own unique backgrounds.

Do not overlook immigrant parents who have lived in another culture and can provide an exciting and interesting program by simply discussing their lives in their homelands. Fellow students who have come from other countries and are comfortable speaking with class members can be invited to make a presentation or to visit and chat informally about their experiences in both cultures.

In many communities with one or more ethnic neighborhoods, community and senior centers have programs which are attended by groups of people who have come from other countries and meet at the center to maintain contact with their friends. (These groups are usually listed in the telephone directory under the society name and can also be located by calling the local Chamber of Commerce. Owners of ethnic businesses such as restaurants often support such organizations as well and can direct interested parents to the group office or knowledgeable sponsor.) Gatherings may center around specific activities such as flower arranging, other arts and crafts, or skills or the people may just get together to chat and reminisce. Ethnic heritage associations such as the Italian-American Society, the Lugo-American Society, and many others also meet regularly and might be enthusiastic about supporting second language classes. If a parent or teacher takes time to ask by stopping by a community center in person or by posting notices on community bulletin boards or in organization newsletters, many of these people would enjoy sharing their talents or memories with young students. Explaining that volunteers will be talking to children in an informal setting can help overcome any initial hesitancy. And a field trip to a center where students can observe and/or participate in an activity such as a songfest, folk dancing, or food preparation would be fun for children and adults alike.

One very worthwhile project which can be undertaken on a small or large scale by any number of parents is expanding the collection in the school library with materials in the second language. Fiction and nonfiction books at many age levels as well as booklets, records, and films can be acquired through purchase or by donations. Sponsoring a fund raiser to benefit the school library can also draw on the support of working parents who are unable to help during the day but would welcome the chance to make a contribution to their child's language program.

With a slightly different focus, parents interested in providing a second language curriculum for their children can be especially effective in winning support for a program from other parents and teachers in the school PTA or parent booster group. Sometimes starting with one or two enthusiastic parents who might encourage a school-wide international dinner is enough to spark interest from others. Emphasizing the world community on holidays which are widely celebrated such as Christmas, New Year's, and International Children's Day could be a starting point for those wanting to stimulate discussion of a new program.

Recruiting new students for ongoing programs is often effective merely by making people aware that the programs exist and that children receive many benefits by growing up bilingual. One parent prepared a slide and tape presentation of a mother talking to her little girl about their heritage. As they went through the family album, the mother pointed out her own parents and talked to her daughter about what it must have been like growing up in another land. The child began to realize how different her grandparents' lives had been from her own, and she wanted to know more about the culture she came from. Speaking the traditional language was one way she could become closer to her grandparents and her heritage. That beautiful presentation was used by the school district as a simple, effective tool to spark parental enthusiasm in the world language program.

One other way that parents can enrich the second language experience is by providing opportunities for their children to continue using that language during breaks in the school year. One or two families with minimal advance planning can host an informal backyard pot-luck during a school break. With more time and effort, parents can join together to set up a full scale language camp over the summer vacation. The site of this camp can be a backyard or the local park. In certain parts of the country, formal language camps are offered to help students develop and maintain skills when school is not in session. Of course, budget and the amount of parental time and effort available will determine which course is best. In my own community, several of us hired a teacher and worked with her to plan activities in a day camp setting. We included games, cooking, crafts, singing, and occasional films obtained from the local library. Though the teacher directed the program, we parents did much of the advance planning. Though our focus was on recreational activities, we just as easily could have designed an academically oriented program.

So, by all means issue an enthusiastic invitation to all of the parents, whatever their level of skill in the classroom language, to contribute in any way they can to extend the learning experience for their children. Many are eager to help and wait to hear that they are welcome.

Parents in the Community

Often those parents who are most active working with the teachers to enrich the second language program are the ones who made the community aware of the need for such a program in the first place. In many parts of the United States, second language education began in community after-school programs initiated and staffed completely by parents. Even when they have not actually provided the instruction, parents have frequently been the motivating force behind getting a program started in the schools.

Often renewed interest in an existing program is generated by school activities which focus on students in that program and what they are learning. Keeping a low profile is definitely not the way to build interest in world language studies! Parents who make sure that the special needs of those students are known by administrators and other parents who might make spending decisions are particularly valuable and need to know that.

Linda McHenry, a California mother, was instrumental in establishing a Spanish immersion program in her local school district. At first, she spent time researching second language teaching methods and the effectiveness of immersion programs. After she was sure of the program she wanted for her children's school, she began a campaign to educate and persuade local parents and school board members that the program was worthwhile and viable in their area. Because of her tireless effort and dedication, the Davis (CA) schools have had a thriving Spanish immersion program for the past five years. An enthusiastic parent support group raises funds to add books to the library and to send the language teachers to conferences and seminars.

In Edmond (OK), Jan Barrick was the Special Programs Administrator for the public school district. She cooperated with interested parents to set up programs teaching world languages before and after the normal school day. Although the instruction is provided in regular classrooms, there is no cost to the school district because the teaching is done by bilingual members of the community. Often these teachers are mothers who want their children to learn the second language and enjoy teaching because they have their own youngsters in the classroom. This program has been so successful that when Jan moved to another city, she persuaded the school board to let her initiate the program there as well. Costs of running the program are covered by small student fees, and response is growing in the community. The initial program has been in effect for over eight years, the second one was begun six years ago, and within the past three years the program has been adopted by several other Oklahoma school districts.

Another important community program is after school and vacation activities at neighborhood parks and recreation centers. Parents can talk to the city director of parks and recreation or to the director of the local YMCA or community center to set up arts and crafts classes or regular organized games where the world language is used by counselors. This would be especially appropriate where there is an ethnic community using that language nearby. Children from the language program could mix easily with native speaking children to the advantage of both. But the desirability of such community sponsored activities is often overlooked by administrators and planners. Parents must approach them to make known the need for such services and to offer support and assistance in getting the programs started.

Making their voices heard by the federal and state legislators is another important contribution parents can make. Funding for education is often decided in the political arena, and voters who raise their voices on an issue usually gain the attention of those who make the decisions. That is a key reason why it is especially important to have an organized body of advocates for second language education. An officer of the group can be assigned the responsibility for tracking legislative affairs and can bring current issues and pending bills to the attention of the group membership. This information is available from the foreign language consultants in the state department of education or from the office of the locally elected representative. Often legislators, especially at the state level, are very willing to speak to special interest groups not only to present their own positions on issues, but primarily to find out what their constituents consider to be important priorities. Parents should remember that the elected officials have been voted into office to work on behalf of the community and to serve its needs.

Another way that parents can work to support second language programs is to become regular correspondents with their legislators. Letters from voters on specific issues such as bills adding second language requirements to the elementary school curriculum are a powerful statement to lawmakers on the priorities of their constituents. And letter writing campaigns in support of pending bills in the area of educational funding are another way parents can be influential. Many times parents are very willing to offer their support if they know it is needed. Making them aware of what they can do in this area is frequently overlooked, yet their voices are the very ones which can influence the vote. Rather than involving teachers and administrators in political matters, the parent advocacy organization can take the initiative in sending home information about pending educational issues in the state legislature. Once again, the message is to keep parents informed.

Conclusion

In summary, parents are their children's most valuable advocates for educational excellence. Teachers need to recognize the importance of parents as a force for effecting change and giving support. We must make the investment now to reap the dividends of a multilingual society. Developing and sustaining a world language program can be accomplished most effectively with committed and enthusiastic parents working alongside dedicated teachers for the benefit of our children and our world.

Resources

Individuals and Organizations

Madeline M. Ehrlich
Advocates for Language Learning
Box 4964
Culver City, CA 90231
213-397-2448

Linda McHenry
330 11th Street
Davis, CA 95616
Information about parent initiated second language program in public schools

Jan Barrick
Education Enrichment Programs
618 SE 27th Street
Edmond, OK 73034
Information about community provided bilingual instruction

Booklists

Nancy Rhodes
Center for Applied Linguistics
118 22nd Street NW
Washington, DC 20037
"Resources for immersion and FLES programs"

American Library Association
"Booklist"
Obtain through local public library
Monthly publication contains book reviews of children's literature in foreign languages

Publishers

Barron's Education Series
113 Crossways Park Drive
Woodbury, NY 11797

Bradbury Press
20 Overhill Road
Scarsdale, NY 10583

Harper & Row Publishers
10 E 53rd Street
New York, NY 10022

William Morrow & Company
105 Madison Avenue
New York, NY 10016

Viking Press, Inc.
625 Madison Avenue
New York, NY 10022

Mail-order Sources

Children's Book & Music Center
Box 1130
Santa Monica, CA 90406
800-443-1856 outside California
213-829-0215 inside California
Books, tapes, records, and games in several languages
Catalog available

Europa Bookstore
3229 N Clark
Chicago, IL 60657
Books in French, German, and Spanish

National Textbook
4255 W Touhy Avenue
Lincolnwood, IL 60646
Textbooks and storybooks in several languages

Selchow & Righter
2215 Union Boulevard
Bayshore, NY 11706
Games in French, German, and Spanish

Foreign Exchange

Youth Exchange
Pueblo, CO 81009
Booklet—"One Friendship at a Time: Your Guide to International Youth Exchange"

Exchange Network of Northern California
312 Sutter Street, Suite 610
San Francisco, CA 94108
415-956-4074
Pamphlet—"International Youth Exchange Guide"

Reading Material and Books

Krashen, S. D.
Inquiries and Insights: Second Language Teaching Immersion and Bilingual Education Literacy
Alemany Press (1985)
Division of Janus Book Publishers, Inc.
2501 Industrial Parkway West
Hayward, CA 94545
415-887-7070

Dolson, D.
Studies on Immersion Education: A Collection for United States Educators
California State Department of Education (1984)
Publications
Box 271
Sacramento, CA 95802
$5.00 per copy must be sent with order

Curtain, H. A., Lipton, G. C., and Rhodes, N. C.
The Many Faces of Foreign Language in the Elementary Schools: FLES, FLEX, and Immersion
American Association of Teachers of French (1985)
57 E Armory
Champaign, IL 61820
$5.00 per copy

Andersson, T.
A Guide to Family Reading in Two Languages: The Preschool Years
National Clearinghouse for Bilingual Education (1977)
4334 Farragut Street
Hyattsville, MD 20781
800-647-0123
$1.25 per copy

Slevin Pirz, T.
Speak French to Your Baby and *Speak Spanish to Your Baby*
Chou-Chou Press (1982, 1985)
Box 152
Shoreham, NY 11786
$14.95 plus handling per book; accompanying tapes available @ $12.95 per set

Vines, L.
A Guide to Language Camps in the U.S.
Harcourt Brace Jovanovich, International
Orlando, FL 32887
$8.00 per copy, includes postage

CAROLYN E. HODYCH was born in Ontario and is now living in Newfoundland. She is the mother of two children in a French immersion program and has been very active in Canadian Parents for French, having served as national president of the organization and currently serving as regional president for Newfoundland and Labrador. She has been chairman of the national publications committee for CPF and is chairman of the editorial board of *More French — S'il vous plaît*, the basic textbook for the French immersion program.

Canadian Parents for French is an organization which has grown to a membership of 16,000 with a strong influence on French immersion programs in Canada and the United States.

Carolyn E. Hodych

Canadian Parents for French: Parent Action and Second Official Language Learning in Canada

Introduction

The theme of this publication is central to what Canadian Parents for French does so well. While our specific aim is to support the learning of French as a second language in Canada, where French and English are the official languages, our major vehicle for getting there is cooperative effort between parents and educators—the vast majority of whom are teachers.

A school board's budgetary, staffing, and administrative concerns leave little time for the consideration of programs actually taught in the schools and less time than desired for considering the well-being of those who are the system's clients. Parents must regularly bring their concerns to the attention of school trustees and other officials responsible for our education system. No other group is going to do this for us. Active participation by parents does sometimes make an educator's job more complicated, but in the end this participation makes the system more responsive. In turn, involved parents are more enthusiastic about their children's education. Children sense this involvement in and support for their education and are more responsive to and interested in the entire process.

Parents are also keenly aware that children should be educated to function not only in today's world but also in the world as it will be 20 to 30 years from now. This explains the current interest in second languages. English may well be the Latin of the twentieth century. However, the Western world is now more multilingual than it was 20 years ago. This trend is likely to continue. We would like our children to be able to participate fully in an increasingly multilingual world. It is toward this goal we strive.

Historical Background

The French and English languages have coexisted over much of the geographical expanse now known as Canada since this area was settled by Europeans. That both languages should have the right to coexist was first recognized in the Treaty of Paris of 1763 which ceded New France to Britain but retained the right of the French-speaking residents to laws and education in their own language. The Constitution Act of 1867 again guaranteed equal status for the French and English languages, as did the Manitoba Act of 1870 and the Official Language Act of 1969. These constitutional guarantees were further reinforced in the Canadian Charter of Rights and Freedoms of 1982.

However, until recently, the reality has been that for many Francophone Canadians and especially for those living outside Quebec, these rights were mostly theoretical and largely ignored.

With the rise of the Quebec independence movement in the 1960s, Anglophone Canadians began to realize that learning the two official languages ought to be the norm rather than the exception available only to a privileged few. Moreover, all children should have the opportunity not only to learn a second language but to learn it in a way that would enable them to speak that second language with confidence. Parents thought this could most easily be accomplished early in life rather than later.

Consequently, in 1965, parents in the St. Lambert area of Montreal proposed that their young children be "immersed" in their second language when they entered school for the first time. They supposed that these children would absorb and come to understand and speak the second language in much the same way as they had learned their first language.

When this French immersion program finally got under way in 1967, an evaluation component was built into the yearly cycle. The results clearly demonstrated that these children could and did learn French with no subsequent loss of ability in English, mathematics, or the sciences.[1]

Word began to spread about the St. Lambert experiment. By 1969, French schools which accepted non-Francophones were flourishing in Toronto, Ontario; Regina, Saskatchewan; and Vancouver, British Columbia. Ottawa, the country's capital city, began its first immersion program in 1970. In addition, parents had begun forming groups in support of their own French programs.

In Canada, education is the responsibility of the provincial and territorial governments. However, because the Federal Government is committed to and responsible for bilingualism, it provides both moral and financial support to the provinces. Through the Department of the Secretary of State of Canada, money for minority language education (English in Quebec, French outside Quebec) and for second official language education has been passed on to the ten provinces and two territories since 1970.[2] This financial support is divided into four general areas:

1 Infrastructure Support — supports ongoing programs and activities in the form of per-student payments and/or special arrangements agreed to bilaterally.

2 Program Expansion and Development — supports the expansion of existing programs and the development and implementation of new ones. These activities are funded on a cost-shared basis (usually 50-50).

3 Teacher Training and Development — provides for bursaries and workshops, funded at 100 percent by the Federal Government.

4 Student Support — provides for bursaries, exchanges, and immersion sessions, funded at 100 percent by the Federal Government.

While these funds do not cover all costs of second official language education they do provide a strong incentive for the provinces and territories to develop and maintain second language programs.

All provinces and territories support French second language programs with some of their own money in addition to the funds which come to them through the federal/provincial agreements. All provinces and territories have ministries of education which receive the money for French language education. This money must be used in an agreed-upon way and public documentation must be provided to show how this money is spent.

Origins of Canadian Parents for French

In addition to the important support provided by the Department of the Secretary of State, the pursuit of bilingualism in Canada is greatly facilitated by the support and resources of the Office of the Commissioner of Official Languages, established in 1970 as part of the Official Languages Act. The Commissioners, three have held office to date, are advocates of language reform; and they promote and encourage linguistic equality for both of Canada's official languages. The Commissioner of Official Languages reports directly to Parliament each year on progress toward equal status for French and English in Canada.

It was through the good offices of the first Commissioner of Official Languages that Canadian Parents for French was formed. For the first five of his seven-year term, Keith Spicer had been observing the actions taken by the Federal Government to make Canada truly bilingual. A number of these initiatives involved teaching French to members of the civil service. At the same time he was witnessing the birth of French immersion programs and the parent groups which were springing up in support of these programs. Mr. Spicer sensibly concluded that it would be much easier and cheaper to make people bilingual when they were young and in the regular school system. He wondered what would happen if some of these enterprising parents were brought together.

In March of 1977, under the auspices of the Commissioner of Official Languages, 35 parents from across Canada came to Ottawa for a Parents Conference on French Language and Exchange Opportunities. When the weekend was over, Canadian Parents for French had been formed and its three goals enunciated.[3] These three goals were and still are:

- to assist in ensuring that each Canadian child have the opportunity to acquire as great a knowledge of the French language and culture as he or she is willing and able to attain;
- to promote the best possible types of French language learning opportunities; and
- to establish and maintain effective communication between parents and educational and governmental authorities responsible for the provision of French language learning opportunities.

To accomplish these goals, it was proposed that CPF:

1 produce publications popularizing relevant research, case studies, and other pertinent information
2 produce a current directory of resource people, programs, and organizations
3 produce an annotated bibliography of relevant research
4 hold a national parents conference
5 communicate the Association's goals and ideas to appropriate authorities and the general public

During the following months, a small committee drafted the by-laws, started a national newsletter, and organized CPF's first national conference in Ottawa on October 14–16, 1977. Sixty interested people came from across Canada. A board of directors was formed giving equal representation to all provinces and CPF was on its way!

Growth of Canadian Parents for French

Our first five years were difficult and uncertain. CPF at the national level was receiving some funding from the Department of the Secretary of State but this was tentative and unpredictable. However, due to the tenacity of a small core of CPF volunteers, dedication and creative thinking on the part of our tiny and part-time national office staff, constant support from the Commissioner's office, and the vision and support of some people from the Department of the Secretary of State as well as some educators and researchers, CPF was able to remain in existence long enough to develop branches in all provinces and territories and to begin to actively encourage the formation of local chapters in communities where parent groups had not already formed.

By pursuing an internal strategy of building a strong volunteer network of parents[4] and by providing our volunteers with current information on the what, where, why, and how-to of asking for second-language programs,[5] CPF has, after ten years, built a strong and truly national organization which involves our 15,000 individual members at every level of the organization from CPF's 156 local chapters to our ten provincial and two territorial branches to the 16-person national board of directors and CPF's modest office in Ottawa.

It is exceedingly difficult to talk about the energy, dedication, resourcefulness, and sheer ingenuity of so many CPF volunteers without mentioning specific names and relating particular anecdotes. It is these qualities, displayed by many individuals throughout Canada, which have made CPF what it is today. All those separate accomplishments have accumulated into an impressive list.

By pursuing an external strategy of interpersonal contacts which involved working with teachers, principals, administrators, and government officials at all levels, CPF volunteers have been instrumental in the spread of French immersion and extended French[6] programs, in increasing the number of students enrolling in such programs,[7] in heightening the interest in and expectations of traditional French programs,[8] in increasing the opportunities for studying in French at the post-secondary level,[9] in the proliferation of French summer camps,[10] in helping to bring about improvements to teacher training programs,[11] and in a growing recognition of the value of bilingualism.[12]

Looking Ahead!

What are CPF's plans for the future? Basically, more of the same.

Internally, we would like to continue to *broaden our base*. Ideally, there should be a CPF local chapter for every school district in the country. To realize this possibility, CPF must have strong and stable branches at the provincial and territorial level. This will involve the setting up of a permanent office in each province with a small paid staff in order to allow volunteers to continue the public work only they can do while servicing growing numbers of local chapters and coping with the usual administrative tasks that accompany expansion.

Another and increasingly urgent need is *volunteer development and training*. As CPF grows, so grows the need for volunteers skilled in public relations, lobbying, goal setting, program evaluation, and fundraising. We must learn to build volunteer training sessions into as many of our activities as possible in order to provide people with the skills necessary to do the work that needs to be done. Rewards are also important, so we must learn to recognize in a more public way the excellent work done so enthusiastically and generously by countless CPF volunteers.

With the growth of CPF comes the need for *better communications* between groups at all levels of the organization. An important component of CPF's growth has been the personal contacts which develop and the feeling of moral support generated at conferences and meetings. Not only do we learn facts and techniques but we can talk to other interested and experienced people from other communities and provinces about our own personal theories or about problems being experienced personally by our children or in our schools. Always we find sympathy and often good practical advice as well. The result is a strengthening of our desire to keep on trying. We must continue to ensure that the opportunities for making such personal contacts continue to be possible even as our organization grows larger.

In addition we must improve the flow of information among the three levels within CPF. Local chapters and individual voluntary efforts are the life blood of CPF. However, working in isolation is very unrewarding and often futile. Local groups need the information, contacts, and tactical help that can only be provided at the provincial and national level. The provincial and national levels need the constant pressure which can only be applied effectively by small groups in individual communities. Only when all three levels work together can we convince governmental authorities that the requests being made at the provincial and national levels are indeed supported by the voting public across Canada.

Our greatest concern for the future is *funding*. The continued funding provided by the Federal Government has been very important to the survival and success of CPF. Progress would have been much slower if most of our energies over the last 10 years had been directed at fundraising from public sources. However, we do feel vulnerable in being heavily dependent upon one source of funds. In addition, many of the needs we see as vitally important to attaining our objectives are ineligible for government funding—certain staff salaries being the best example. We must develop a realistic and more successful fundraising strategy if we are to expand as we hope to.

Externally, CPF aims to:

- ensure continued moral and financial support by the Federal Government for the teaching of both official languages
- support and work to improve existing French second language learning programs
- initiate programs in areas where none now exist
- help explain the need for such programs to administrators, teachers, and parents who continue to need information about second language learning
- increase the opportunities to study in French at the post-secondary level
- initiate more and better research into the learning of second languages
- continue to build on the cooperation that has developed between CPF and Francophone groups across Canada

Tens of thousands of parents in Canada believed in bilingualism in 1974. CPF provided a channel through which these people could get information on what programs were available, how to introduce these programs into their communities, and how to support existing programs. CPF also gave them access to a network of contacts through which they could get moral and tactical support as well as advice on specific problems. There will be a need for this kind of support for second language programs in Canada for a long time. Canadian Parents for French intends to continue providing that leadership as long as the need exists.

Notes

1 For an overview of recent findings see Lapkin, S., & Swain, M. Research update. *Language and Society*, 1984, *12 Winter*, 48–54.

2 For a complete description of the support which comes to the provinces/territories from the Federal Government for the teaching of French as a second language, please refer to the minutes of the Standing Joint Committee of the Senate and the House of Commons on Official Languages. The minutes of May 14, 1986 (Issue #30) contain Mark Goldenberg's excellent description of these bilateral agreements. Complete financial details for the 1983–84 to 1985–86 agreements are contained in Appendix "OLLO-14" of the June 4, 1986 minutes (Issue #33). Both sets of minutes can be obtained from the Canadian Government Publishing Centre, Supply and Services Canada, Ottawa, Canada K1A 0S9.

3 CPF's original mandate and immediate concerns were well documented in the first *CPF National Newsletter*, June 1977. A few copies are still available from the CPF National Office, 309 Cooper St., Suite 210, Ottawa, Ontario, Canada K2P 0G5.

4 This is mainly accomplished in two ways. First, through its publications and publicity work CPF encourages interested people, both parents and teachers, to come to a CPF meeting or conference and begin to be involved through what they learn and whom they meet there. Second, interested parents or teachers are encouraged to ask CPF to send a representative to talk to groups of potentially interested parents.

5 CPF devotes considerable energy to the development and production of a full range of informational material. The pamphlets "What is core French?", "What is extended French?", "What is early French immersion?", "What is late French immersion?", and "What is continuing French immersion?" describe the range of programs currently available. In addition to these and other pamphlets, CPF has published two books, *So you want your child to learn French!*, which contains a great deal of self-help and how-to information for parents, and *More French, s'il vous plait!*. The *CPF Immersion Registry* which lists and describes all French immersion programs in Canada is produced annually. In addition, CPF has developed a "Resources List" which contains references to research papers, briefs, reports, and presentations which provide information parents may find useful in asking for new or improved language programs. For the full list of CPF publications, write to the CPF National Office, 309 Cooper St., Suite 210, Ottawa, Ontario, K2P 0G5.

6 Extended French programs involve at least 40 minutes per day of instruction in basic French as well as another subject (for example, history, science, mathematics, or geography) taught in French.

7 The spread of French immersion programs in Canada is well documented annually by *The CPF Immersion Registry* and in the Commissioner of Official Languages' annual reports which are available from the Communications Branch, Office of the Commissioner of Official Languages, Ottawa, Ontario, Canada K1A 0T8. In 1977–78 a total of 237 schools in Canada offered French immersion programs and involved 37,881 students. By 1985–86 the number of schools offering the program had increased to 1,143, enrolling 177,824 students (Commissioner of Official Languages, Annual Report 1985, p. 228).

8 In Canada, traditional French programs, often called "core" or "basic" French, are roughly the equivalent of FLEX programs in the United States. In the past, these programs have been mostly grammar oriented and generally have not concentrated on producing communicative competence in French. Recently, however, both teachers and parents have been interested in experimenting with these programs to try to achieve greater communicative competence. J. Clarence LeBlanc's article "Is core French a valid option?" in W. R. McGillivray (Ed.), *More French, s'il vous plait!* Ottawa, Ont.: CPF, 1986, provides a good summary of current thinking.

CPF also commissioned and recently published a survey: *Core French in Canada. Volume 1, A survey of programs; Volume 2, A guide to resources*, which was edited by Janet Poyen with the assistance of Judy Gibson and is available from the CPF National Office. Volume 2 is particularly interesting because it describes developments in core French and the creative use of local resources throughout Canada.

9 During the past year and a half, CPF has hosted a series of regional conferences and one national meeting on French at the post-secondary level. With the number of students involved in French immersion programs nearing 200,000, parents are anxious that universities, community colleges, and other post-secondary institutions be prepared to meet the needs of students who wish to continue to pursue bilingualism at the post-secondary level and in subject areas other than French.

10 CPF volunteers have been increasingly involved with setting up and running summer French camps for both immersion and non-immersion students. Some of these programs are described in our "Summer programs in French" booklet, available from the CPF National Office in Ottawa.

11 Teacher training and teacher supply are of great concern. CPF has been working toward improved second language teacher training programs for some years and improvements are beginning to take place. During 1985–86, two new teacher training programs (University of New Brunswick and University of Regina) and two teacher retraining programs (Simon Fraser University and University of Victoria) have begun.

12 In 1984, CPF commissioned a poll by the Gallup organization which showed that 2 out of 3 Canadians wanted their children to learn French in order to become bilingual. Since then, two other polls commissioned by a Montreal newspaper and the "Societe franco-manitobaine" in Winnipeg, and a national poll conducted by the Commissioner of Official Languages have confirmed a continuing high level of public support for bilingualism.

BADI G. FOSTER, President of the Ætna Institute for Corporate Education (AEtna Life and Casualty), previously held several positions at Harvard University, first as a lecturer in education in the Harvard Graduate School of Education and then as Assistant Director of the John F. Kennedy Institute of Politics. He has also been a visiting professor in the Afro-American Studies Department at Harvard.

Mr. Foster received his Ph.D. from Princeton University and wrote his dissertation on the Moroccan power structure. He then remained on the staff at Princeton as Chairman of the Afro-American Studies Program.

The author of more than 25 articles, many of which explore the collaboration between higher education and corporate education, Mr. Foster has served as a consultant for universities, foundations, and government agencies.

In addition to his widely recognized expertise in corporate education, he is well known for his research on the Muslim Arab world. Mr. Foster speaks French and Moroccan Arabic.

Badi G. Foster

The Role of the Foreign Language Teacher in American Corporate Education

Introduction

The American corporation has become increasingly sophisticated in its approach to managing its workforce. Education has played a significant role in this approach. The American corporation has also been faced with increasing international concerns, which have required the corporation to think globally and act locally. Some corporations have been adjusting to an international perspective. Others have failed to recognize the need to adjust.

Foreign language teachers may serve as a catalyst to change the perspective of American corporations and shape the future of American business.

The Emergence of Corporate Education

American business has moved from looking at employees as an expense to seeing them as an investment.

In the past, corporations viewed employees as a cost. Labor was often nameless and faceless doing undifferentiated work. Time and motion studies were the projects of choice among organizational experts of fledgling management schools, such as Harvard, Wharton and Chicago. The worker was viewed as another cog in the machinery of the Industrial Age. This view was epitomized by the film "Modern Times," in which Chaplin vainly attempts to keep pace in the modern workplace.

This view of the worker has changed. Authors such as John Naisbitt (1983) have chronicled the end of the Industrial Age. Society has moved to an information age with service-based economies. Organizational experts in schools of management are discussing employee needs and how organizations are fulfilling those needs; such as, the Maslowian objective of self-actualization.

The emphasis of the employee as a resource due to the shift from manual to knowledge work was highlighted by Peter Drucker in a recent *Wall Street Journal* article.

> Even in the smokestack industries the manual-labor component of the work force accounts for no more than a quarter by now. In most other industries it is down to one-sixth or less. Productivity of white-collar workers and especially of the rapidly

growing groups of knowledge workers is thus the central productivity challenge in all developed countries. But knowledge-worker productivity is far less a matter of quantity of output than of quality. Few things are less productive than an engineer turning out with great skill, great enthusiasm and great diligence masses of drawings for the wrong product. And the critical factors in the productivity of knowledge work are such things as attitudes, adequate information, work flow, job relationships and the design of jobs and teams. Above all productivity in knowledge work is dependent on putting into the job the person with the right performance strengths for the assignment.

As Drucker points out, several of the keys to productivity are adequate information, attitudes, and job relationships. The process of educating assists in the development of these keys. More explicitly, corporate heads are realizing the value of the investment in education and the link to productivity. As John Filer, former Chairman of ÆEtna Life and Casualty, has said, "The resource that will most clearly distinguish us from others, over time, is our people. In the composite their education, training, motivation, resourcefulness, mobility, flexibility, and sense of well-being and achievement will determine our success as a nation and our opportunities for success as individuals and business executives."

A company's productivity and business growth depend on the quality of its employees. The educational process insures that quality. As Mills (1985) has demonstrated, there is a positive correlation between successful corporations and corporations that manage their human resources well.

One model of a corporation addressing business issues through education has been the creation of the ÆEtna Institute for Corporate Education. The Institute provides a variety of programs from basic entry level to advanced managerial and technical training. In order to meet the many kinds of educational needs of ÆEtna's diverse workforce, the Institute draws on the resources of many other providers of education including schools, colleges, external consultants, and professional associations.

Over 250 programs are offered on a continuing basis covering executive, management, and supervisory education; individualized skills development; and career education. Many programs deal with needs common to employees in all divisions of the corporation, but programs are also tailored to meet the specific needs of one or more area.

Most companies have an educational function similar to the Institute's and they make substantial investments in corporate education. In a Carnegie Foundation study several years ago, the annual expenditure for corporate education in the United States was conservatively estimated as exceeding forty billion dollars (Eurich, 1982). As Ernest Boyer, President of the Carnegie Foundation for the Advancement of Teaching, points out, that figure is "...approaching the total annual expenditures of all of America's four-year and graduate colleges and universities. And the number of employees involved in corporate education may equal the total enrollment in those same institutions — nearly 8 million students" (Eurich, 1985, ix.).

With the increasing view of the employee as a valuable asset, corporations have adopted some form of corporate education. Corporate education has taken a significant role in meeting and shaping the objectives of the organization.

As dramatic as these changes have been, the American corporation faces continuing change. One significant change will be the requirement for American corporations to assume an international perspective and to manage cultural diversity.

The Global Economy

Robert Reich in *The Next American Frontier* (1983) has provided an argument for the development of a national industrial policy. In so doing, he outlines the links of the larger global economy. Increasingly, American corporations are influenced by international activities and international affairs. As consumers we have been sensitive to the world price of oil and its relationship to our personal comfort and mobility. American automotive workers have been sensitive to the balance of trade agreements with foreign auto manufacturers. American financiers have been sensitive to the growing debt in developing nations. Clearly, these relationships seem quite straightforward and are explicit in their international link.

A more subtle international link has been developed with American corporations absorbing international businesses and international businesses absorbing American corporations. This has created multinational conglomerates which have a transnational economic influence. The number of international or multinational conglomerates continues to grow (Vansina, 1975). The growth of these conglomerates has an immediate economic effect both domestically and internationally.

Fest and Robbins (1976) have provided several examples of this international corporate link. In Belgium, forty-eight percent of the largest 120 corporations are controlled wholly or in part from abroad. American companies control ninety percent of Europe's microcircuit production. With the exception of Germany, South Carolina has the largest amount of German capital investment in the world.

Often corporations have considered some international aspect to their business. Planning departments with econometric modeling factor international variables. Financial departments consider exchange rates. Marketing departments consider alternatives to the domestic market. American businesses, however, may be unaware of their international connections. For example, at a large insurance meeting in the Midwest, the discussion was raised about reinsurance—the process by which a portion of the risk is sold to another company. Most of those in attendance were shocked to find the major reinsurance broker which held their policies was a corporation in Bulgaria.

Through international affairs and multinational corporations, American business is linked to a larger global economy. Consequently, American corporations require an international perspective.

The American Corporate International Perspective

As American business has grown in the global economy, the need for an international or multinational perspective for the American business person has increased. The failure of corporations to appreciate or develop this perspective has provided colorful stories for dinner conversation. Stories abound of the executive faux pas in international settings. Entertaining as these stories may be, the problems generated by the lack of an international perspective or an understanding of cultural diversity leads to a tremendous waste of organizational resources. Schnapper (1977, p. 3) provides several examples.

- A Venezuelan vice-president of marketing for an American-owned multinational is fired by the president because he refuses a promotion, which would mean abandoning his parents in Caracas and moving to Boston. In Venezuela where children are expected to take care of their parents, "abandoning them" would be shameful. The American president of the company is angered and confused by the Latin American "lack of appreciation and loyalty."

- A German engineer, thinking he has successfully negotiated a joint venture with a Japanese firm returns home to await the Japanese signatures of the contract, and discovers several weeks later, that the Japanese have not agreed to over half of the contractual conditions. While he was in Tokyo, the Japanese smiled and nodded approvingly all during his presentations. They also wined and dined him very graciously, and never hinted at being resistant to his proposal. He had no idea that during the brief time of their acquaintance, they were not yet ready to disclose their serious reservations.

- A sale of millions of tons of wheat to the Soviet government results in severe price increases for bread in the U.S. The U.S. businessmen, in their eagerness to close a profitable deal, assumed that once the major agreement was finished, they and their Soviet counterparts would work out the fine details quickly and with little difficulty. Later on, the Americans found themselves yielding on many minor aspects of the total agreement because the Russian negotiators went over the contract with painstaking thoroughness, and were ready to cancel the whole contract, based on an impasse over any one of these fine points.

These types of cross-cultural misunderstandings occur frequently in the corporate community. Such misunderstandings undermine a company's productivity, and productivity in corporate America has been under attack. Several organizational authors, the most popular being Peters and Waterman (1982), have assailed the issue of productivity in American corporations.

If productivity in corporate America is linked to gaining an international perspective and understanding cultural diversity, why then have corporations been slow to recognize the need for multicultural training?

Two reasons predominate: one, the complexity of the organization; and two, the ethnocentricity of corporate executives.

C. Wickham Skinner (1964) provides a model of the four domains which influence managerial philosophy and practice (see Figure 1).

One readily sees the complexity of these intermeshing systems in one culture and one language. Now consider multiple systems of multiple cultures and multiple languages. Add subcultures to the picture and one sees the difficulty in operating in such a diverse context or managing such a diverse organization. Overwhelmed by such complexity, some executives avoid the issue of dealing with diversity by not addressing it.

More often, American executives don't recognize the complexity of cultural diversity or the potential problems associated in the multicultural setting; until, as demonstrated by the previous examples, they are reflecting on what went wrong. The ethnocentric response to multicultural issues by American executives is broad. Some executives believe their approach to an issue is the preferred approach with little room for considered alternatives. They see no reason why they should learn anything new about language or culture. Others approach multicultural issues with tokenism. They may learn several phrases or read a book and make an initial step at learning the culture. Others may learn the language and study the culture but never shift from an academic appreciation to understanding or empathy even though they may be world traveled.

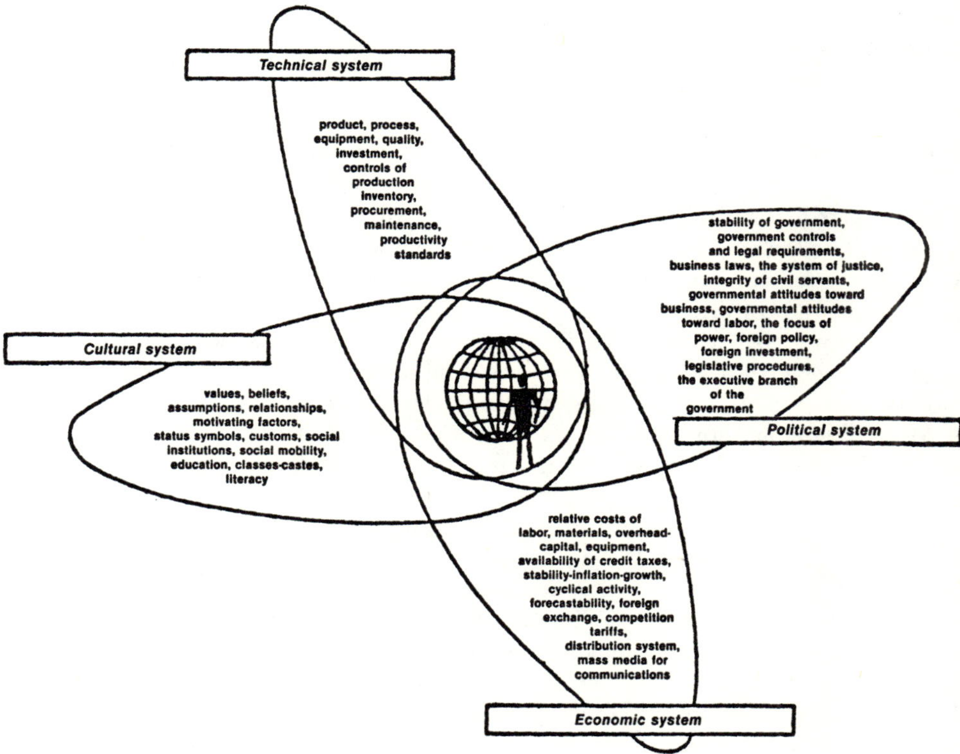

Figure 1. Four intermeshing systems which influence managerial philosophy and practice.

(From "Management of international production" by C. W. Skinner. *Harvard Business Review*, September–October 1964, *42*, 132.)

Regardless of an executive's position on the ethnographical spectrum, often single language executives with little multicultural experience pale in the multilingual business setting. To compensate, American executives may throw money or power into the setting which leads to images of the "ugly American."

More corporations need to develop an international perspective with an understanding of cultural diversity. Some corporations are looking overseas to find managers to fulfill this requirement. As Pat Choate, Director of Human Resources for TRW, recently said, "For the next generation of leaders in American corporations; we should go overseas to hire them." Obviously, hiring overseas creates its own set of problems. It does, however, address the question, how do we educate the future leaders and current leaders of American business to think globally and act locally? Foreign language teachers are in a unique position to serve as a catalyst for change in corporate America's thinking.

Approaching Change

Thomas Kuhn (1962) in *The Structure of Scientific Revolutions* introduced the term "paradigm shift." A paradigm shift occurs when one's frame of reference or view of reality changes. For example, in Newtonian physics, nature had order and absolutes. When Einstein introduced his theory of relativity, the natural laws became relative. Such a change shifted the way a person viewed the world and his or her relationship to it. As Kuhn (1962) pointed out, every significant breakthrough in science was a break with a current pattern of thinking or perception of reality.

It is the current pattern of thinking in American corporations that needs to be changed. Many managers try to manage an international or multinational firm as if it were a national firm on a grander scale, by applying old solutions to new problems (Vansina, 1975). The paradigm for American executives needs to shift from a national perspective managing cultural homogeneity to a multinational perspective managing cultural diversity.

Language instruction provides an excellent starting point to introduce such a paradigm shift, but language is just a starting point. For example, an industrious executive from an American high tech corporation learned Japanese in order to conduct business for the company in Japan. In discussing a large sale, the executive, with his Japanese counterpart, determined their thinking was "parallel" on quantity and price. After placing the order, the American awaited the final contract documents. When they did not arrive the American returned to his counterpart and discussed the order. Indeed, they had discussed that their thinking had been "parallel" on quantity and price. For the American, the interpretation of parallel meant thinking alike and in agreement, thus the executive placed the order. For the Japanese, the interpretation of parallel meant two ideas stretching into infinity that would never meet, thus, for him no agreement was reached and the purchase fell through. This misunderstanding transcended language. What was required was to look at the term in cultural context and to verify intent.

In the previous examples of the Venezuelan vice-president, the German engineer, and the Soviet wheat deal, language per se was not an issue. Although the examples do not provide knowledge of the participants' language capabilities, what led to misunderstanding and error was the lack of cultural appreciation and understanding. Learning a foreign language is a natural conduit for deeper cultural appreciation and contextual understanding. Such an objective, however, challenges the foreign language teacher to push beyond traditional foreign language learning objectives.

Along all points of the educational continuum, from preschool through adult education programs, the need exists to develop a greater understanding of cultural diversity. Education, in its variety of forms, provides the framework for change to create the paradigm shift, in the thinking of current and future leaders of corporate America. Foreign language teachers may become the most effective change agents in creating the shift by assuming a position of leadership in the community. Leadership not limited to specific role or title, rather foreign language teachers may lead by providing direction, drive, and vision in meeting community needs.

At the preschool, elementary, and secondary levels, foreign language teachers should search for opportunities to present language and cultural programs and lobby for such programs with the attending allocation of resources. Teachers should serve as role models to instill the value of a foreign language and cultural understanding to an impressionable youth.

At the college and university level, undergraduate and graduate programs abound in language, area studies, and study abroad programs. One area that has not had as much focus has been preparation to operate in an international or multinational business. Often students, in declaring a major, are locked into departmental requirements which do not encourage a broad approach to language, culture, and business. Only now are graduate programs in business beginning to appreciate the international dimension to American business with scattered offerings in the curriculum.

The traditional programs that have merged language with area studies such as the School for Advanced International Studies at The Johns Hopkins University or the Fletcher School of Law and Diplomacy of Tufts University have predominantly prepared students for careers in diplomatic service. One institution offering a program that has merged language, cultural, and business training is the American School for International Management commonly known as "Thunderbird." Although graduates of this program have attained distinguished positions in business internationally and although the program enjoys an excellent reputation, it has remained somewhat of an anomaly on the American corporate landscape, which prefers hiring the traditional MBA. Foreign language instructors at this level should seek out opportunities for joint programs or promote programs which include language and cultural studies as a component of a business degree.

The field of corporate education and foreign language instruction has a sporadic history at best. Often an interest in language is a two-week introductory approach initiated by executives on their way to a foreign assignment. Some corporations have orientations to foreign assignments lasting from two to four hours to two to four days. More corporations are starting to realize the international nature of their work and are incorporating training with an international perspective and ongoing language training into their educational programs. Others are starting to address the nature of the multinational corporation and trying to deal with cultural diversity within the organization.

As education becomes an increasingly important concern on the public agenda and as corporations commit more resources to training and education, the foreign language teacher serves a critical role in articulating the vision of cultural diversity to the community. The concepts that have been briefly introduced in traditional academic settings probably have a familiar ring; however, the corporate educational environment may be unfamiliar. How does a foreign language teacher from an academic setting influence change in the thinking of current leadership in corporate America?

A Strategy for Corporate Educational Collaboration

The strategy for foreign language teachers to influence change in the corporate environment is fourfold. First, the foreign language teacher needs preparation to operate in the corporate environment. Second, the foreign language teacher needs to discover the current business needs of the community. Third, the foreign language teacher needs to meet those business needs. Fourth, after the initial business needs have been met, then the foreign language teacher may provide direction and leadership.

In order to operate in the corporate environment, the foreign language teacher needs to understand the corporate environment. Gaining an understanding of the corporate environment comes from personal preparation by the foreign language teacher. The foreign language teacher needs to communicate in the language of the business community, have an understanding of how businesses operate, and be sensitive to the concerns of business. To do this, the foreign language teacher should become aware of the business environment by reading business publications—from national magazines to the business section of the local papers. One should also attend community activities which provide a forum for the discussion of business issues and also offer opportunities for social interaction. Within the social context, one may learn a great deal about a company's products and organization. Taking business courses at the local college or university will also provide a perspective of the business environment.

Other tangential areas with which the foreign language teacher should have some familiarity are adult learning theories, adult curriculum development models, and management training concepts. Adult learning in a corporate environment, unlike other learning settings, is more issue driven and less instructor driven. Adult learners want material that is relevant and applicable in meeting their problems on the job. By becoming familiar with the business environment and adult learning context, the foreign language teacher may intelligently enter the dialogue in meeting corporate needs.

When business identifies a problem, resources of time, money, and personnel will be applied to solve or alleviate the problem. By entering a dialogue with business, needs will emerge that the foreign language teacher may meet. The needs may not seem readily apparent or even applicable to one's immediate area of expertise. For example, a corporation may need a part-time case writer, instructor, or project manager. Some corporations may have an immediate international or cultural application such as running an orientation program for overseas assignments; others may involve more local issues. Regardless of the specifics, the foreign language teacher gains credibility within the business environment by meeting the corporation's needs and demonstrating that one can operate effectively in that environment.

With experience and credibility, the foreign language teacher may then assume a role of direction and leadership. The foreign language teacher with knowledge of the business may assist in the articulation of problems and anticipate needs within the corporation, which may be met by his or her unique skills. The foreign language teacher thus becomes the in-house expert on international and multicultural training and education. From such a legitimized position, the foreign language teacher has a platform to advocate the importance for the corporation to address international issues and cultural diversity.

Resistance, however, will be inevitable. Schnapper (1977, p. 21) has outlined some of the predominant assumptions which retard multicultural training. He also has provided a contrastive response to those assumptions which may be used by the foreign language teacher to demonstrate the value of multicultural training.

PREDOMINANT ASSUMPTION

"Our people have already proven they can work with people, no matter what their race or culture." Evidence has already demonstrated that the person has proven his intercultural skills by working with a variety of fellow nationals. People are not so radically different, at least on the job.

"Nothing can be done for the person until he is overseas and is in the actual situation." Only the reality of the job situation will produce learning. People will not accept the "reality" of the training situation.

"We're sending mature adults whose basic personality is already set." Mature adults cannot learn or unlearn behaviors even when such changes are to their advantage.

"Our personnel will get along with host nationals by living and working with them." People learn to like each other and work together by being together.

"There is no proof that any kind of preparation makes a difference." This is largely true. Most studies have either evaluated change immediately after training itself, or lacked controls or other "hard research" essentials.

"People are about the same everywhere." People differ only superficially in regard to foods they eat, the language they speak, and the clothes they wear.

CONTRASTIVE RESPONSE

Possessing professional and/or interpersonal skills in one's own country does not guarantee similar success in a different culture. The cultural differences between people are so profound that significant new skills and behaviors are necessary for effective intercultural interaction.

People can learn these new skills and behaviors before they get into the actual setting. Training which emphasizes new behavior in a supportive environment will help the trainee carry these behaviors into a new work situation.

Though the preparatory activity cannot attempt basic personality restructuring, even mature and "set" persons can change and modify their behavior when they see it as serving their purpose. So-called set personality traits such as sensitivity to others, creativity, tolerance for ambiguity, and ability to cope with stress can all be strengthened by a training process.

Working and living with people who are different does not mean that people will learn to love each other or cooperate. There are numerous examples that indicate the contrary.

There are data that effective training can improve the functioning of managers.

Beyond the obvious differences of clothes, physical appearance, and overt behavior are differences of how the world is experienced, of assumptions, and of cognitive structures.

By personal preparation, identifying corporate needs, and meeting those needs, foreign language teachers can assume roles of leadership in influencing the current thinking of corporate America toward a more intercultural perspective.

Conclusion

Some may view the proposal that foreign language teachers may significantly influence corporate America as ambitious. Be that as it may, there are several inescapable dynamics at work in corporate America. First, corporations have identified productivity and the changing business environment as a problem. Managing human resources has been identified as part of the solution. More corporations are committing resources to the training and education of their employees for the future. Second, the global economy is growing. Increasingly American businesses are entering foreign markets and foreign competitors are entering American markets. The phenomenon of the multinational conglomerate is increasing as acquisitions and takeovers increase. Third, the indigenous population of the American workforce is diversified. Increasingly corporate executives have to address the issues of managing a culturally diversified workforce. The dynamics of these forces will not recede with time. Rather, with the known demographic future and inevitable technological advances, they will become of increasing concern to corporate America. Corporations now are starting to address these with varying degrees of urgency.

The question remains who will fill the leadership role in this emerging area. Foreign language teachers are in an excellent position to do so. The skills of communication and cultural understanding which a good foreign language teacher must possess are the same skills which will succeed in a business collaboration. Recently, a group of international development officials gathered to discuss the issues of American collaboration within their countries. The premier problem was not subject or field expertise, rather it was the lack of sensitivity by the Americans to appreciate the cultural context and to communicate effectively. As has been outlined, the same problem exists for corporations which operate internationally, are organized multinationally, or face cultural diversity.

The preparation of future leaders with a multicultural understanding seems well within the scope of foreign language teachers at any level, whether elementary, secondary, or post-secondary. The link between this preparation and future American corporate prosperity has been presented and cannot be overemphasized.

The proposal put forth for foreign language teachers to participate in the development of current corporate leaders is perhaps more ambitious. Not all will consider the challenge. However, those who do will find opportunities for professional growth and personal satisfaction.

References

Drucker, P. Goodbye to the old personnel department. *The Wall Street Journal*, 22 May 1986, 30.

Eurich, N. *Corporate classrooms: The learning business*. Princeton, NJ: Carnegie Foundation for the Advancement of Teaching, 1985.

Fest, T. B., & Robbins, J. G. Cross-cultural communications and the trainer. Monograph prepared for international development session ASTD national convention in New Orleans, LA, 1976.

Kuhn, T. *The structure of scientific revolutions*. 2nd ed., Chicago: University of Chicago Press, 1962.

Mills, D. Q. Planning with people in mind. *Harvard Business Review*, July–August 1985, *63*, 97–105.

Naisbitt, J. *Megatrends*. New York: Warner Books, 1983.

Peters, T. J., & Waterman, R. H. *In search of excellence*. New York: Harper & Row, 1982.

Reich, R. *The next american frontier*. New York: Times Books, 1983.

Schnapper, M. Multinational training for multinational corporations/international organizations. Unpublished monograph, 1977.

Skinner, C. W. Management of international production. *Harvard Business Review*, September–October, 1964, *42*, 125–137.

Vansina, L. S. Improving international relations and effectiveness within multinational organizations. In J. D. Adams (Ed.), *New technologies in organizational development (Vol. 2)*. La Jolla, CA: University Associates, Inc., 1975.

1986 RECIPIENTS OF THE BOARD OF DIRECTORS AWARD FOR EXCELLENCE IN LANGUAGE STUDY

Many secondary schools offer achievement awards to their outstanding students, and the Board of Directors of the Northeast Conference on the Teaching of Foreign Languages feels that more language students should be among those recognized. The following list represents the Awards for Excellence in Language Study presented in 1986. Any school wishing to recognize student achievement by awarding a Board of Directors Award for Excellence in Language Study should contact the Northeast Conference Awards Committee, Box 623, Middlebury, VT 05753, and request a nomination form.

ALASKA
  Conway: **Conway HS**, Elizabeth Thomas (F).
  Palmer: **Palmer HS**, Richard Reader (F).
ARKANSAS
  Fort Smith: **Northside HS**, Maria Kathleen Peloquin (S), Michelle Lee Wewers (F).
CALIFORNIA
  Burlingame: **Mercy HS**, Claudia Bettuchi (S), Claudia Bettuchi (I), Isabel Trouday (F).
  Spreckels: **Spreckels S**, Crystal Stoeberl (F).
COLORADO
  Colorado Springs: **Mitchell HS**, Timothy Klopfer (L), Jeff Peterson (G), Patrick Carter (S), Pascal Lechler (F).
  Denver: **Machebeuf Catholic HS**, Sharon K. Doherty (S).
CONNECTICUT
  Cheshire: **Cheshire HS**, Sanjeev Bhelle (S), Thomas Maxwell (G), Maddaline Orcisco (F), Anna Notation (L).
  Colchester: **Bacon Acad**, Patricia Hogan (S).
  East Hartford: **East Hartford HS**, Sue Rodrigue (F), Beth Minnick (S).
  Glastonbury: **Glastonbury HS**, Paul Swanson (F), Scott Ahlgren (S), George Jennings (R), Francisco Alonso (L). **Gideon Welles JHS**, Larry Cogswell (S), Jeffrey Gilles (R). **Buttonball Elem S**, Matthew Stowe (S). **Eastbury Elem S**, Stephanie Sterling (S). **Hopewell Elem S**, Renu Chhabra (S). **Hebron Avenue Elem S**, Allison Monaco (S). **Naubuc Elem S**, Karen Galinsky (S). **Academy Elem S**, Mark Katibian (S).
  Greenwich: **Greenwich HS**, Eric Smith (S).
  Guilford: **Guilford HS**, Kenneth Close (S), Nhu Ngo (L), Nhu Ngo (F).
  Meriden: **Francis T. Maloney HS**, Roseann Martoreli (I), Mark Blazejowski (L), Christine Daniels (F).
  Naugatuck: **Naugatuck HS**, Katherine Gabrielson (F).
  North Haven: **North Haven HS**, Mila Chun (L), Scott Nabel (S).
  Norwalk: **West Rocks MS**, Jonathan Ablett (F), Katie Bell (S). **Nathan Hale MS**, Kristin Ito (S), Mary Mahanna (F). **Norwalk HS**, Laurel Danelewich (G), Laurie Koteen (F), Rose Carbone (I), Laura Gioiella (S). **Brien McMahon HS**, Maureen Keogh (S), Karen Ortiz (Advanced Hispanos), Marino Sarno (I), Bonnie Wargo (L), Laura DeLuca (F). **Ponus Ridge MS**, Margo Hieronymus (S), Jennifer Oken (F).
  Old Saybrook: **Old Saybrook SHS**, Vincent Cousineau (F), Jim Anton (S). **Main Street S**, Erin Potts (F), Cory Lenz (S).
  Sandy Hook: **Newton HS**, Cathy Sellner (S), Megan McDonald (L), Lisa Phillips (F).
  Stamford: **Sacred Heart Acad**, Amy Manchuck (F), Eileen Conant (S).
  Stratford: **Bunnell HS**, Karen Lavin (F). **Stratford HS**, Marianne Nemec (S).
  West Hartford: **Sedgwick MS**, Amanda Doran (F), Rorie J. Litos (S). **King Philip MS**, Marian Hourdequin (F), Manish Shah (S). **Hall HS**, Thomas Lahiri (G), Yehudah Lindenburg (L), Mochelle Hohnke (S), Linda Carpino (I), Joshua Guenter (F). **Conard HS**, Ken Doran (S), Manuela Mangiafico (F), Manuela Mangiafico (I), Dan Adam (G), Lucille Sheng (Chinese), Elizabeth Joslin (L).
  West Redding: **Joe Barlow HS**, Jenna Donohue (F).

  Wethersfield: **Wethersfield HS**, Amelia Abbruzzese (I), Michael Chesek (S), Jennifer Provost (F). **Silas Deane MS**, Jonathan Danforth (F), Michael Meade (S).
  Wilton: **Wilton HS**, Christopher Cieurzo (G), Carolyn Tracey (S), Jim Morgan (R), Amy Bryan (F).
  Woodbridge: **Amity Reg SHS**, Julie MacRae (S), Arthur Rishi (F), Paul Schrotti (G).
DELAWARE
  Claymont: **Archmere Acad**, Robert M. Kuhar (G), Joseph Hoban (F), Judith Hildick (I), Thomas Ferro (S).
  Dover: **Holy Cross HS**, Raymond Viloria (S), Elizabeth Crahan (F).
DISTRICT OF COLUMBIA
  Washington: **St. Anselm's Abbey S**, David Martin (L), Lawrence Lucier (F), Thomas Cunningham (Greek), Mark Brewer (G).
FLORIDA
  Miami: **Miami Christian C**, Kevin Holman (Hebrew), Stacey Ann Velker (Greek). **Southwood JHS**, Edith Grosse (Hebrew), Mason Ford (S), Maria Tobar (Spanish S), Jeremy Jensen (J), Desiree Rees (L), Vanessa Morales (F).
ILLINOIS
  Chicago: **St. Patrick HS**, David Cordero (F), Tony Sichi (S), David Choate (G).
  Evanston: **Evanston Township HS**, Stephanie Kimmel (F), Kelly Allgaier (G), Erin Ferrill (L), Paul Luning (S).
  Kankakee: **Bishop McNamara HS**, Heather Hoyer (S).
  Libertyville: **Libertyville HS**, Theodore Ts'o (S), Kristine Marie Kayer (F), Brigitta Sorenson (G).
  Mendota: **Mendota HS**, Donna M. Joerger (S).
  Ottawa: **Marquette HS**, Jennifer McCarrens (F).
  Rock Island: **Rock Island HS**, Kristen Kessler (S), David Griffiths (G), Loya DePooter (F).
IOWA
  Mason City: **Mason City HS**, Amy Stroup (S).
  Knoxville: **Nell McGowen JHS**, Scott DeLye (S).
KANSAS
  Kinsley: **Kinsley HS**, Dawn Merritt (F).
  Shawnee Mission: **Shawnee Mission West HS**, Ben Huber (S).
  Witchita: **Witchita Collegiate S**, Deborah Putnam (F).
LOUISIANA
  New Orleans: **Xavier Preparatory HS**, Therese Terrance (F). **Xavier University Prep**, Karen Alcorn (S).
  Lafayette: **Lafayette HS**, Pam Washington (F).
MAINE
  Kennebunk: **Kennebunk HS**, Dawn Christina Jellison (S), Erik Lane Burgess (F), Suzy Shepardson (L), Bernd D. Wolff (G).
  Waldoboro: **Medomak Valley HS**, Steven Dinsmore (F).
  Portland: **Univ. of So Maine**, Mary Lekousi (Greek), Mary Lekousi (L).
MARYLAND
  Annapolis: **Annapolis SHS**, Monica Pinto (S), John Morales (G).
  Baltimore: **Pikesville HS**, Laura McDaniel (F), Debbie Griver (S). **Parksville HS**, Adam Nathanson (S). **Roland Park Country Upper S**, Lisa Krijer (R), Katie O'Donovan (F), Kim Theis (S). **Roland Park Country MS**, Gabrielle Durham (F), Marcy Swingle (L). **Roland Park Country MS**,

Michelle Parker (S).
Burtonsville: Paint Branch HS, Elizabeth Hunt (F), Paul Jeon (L), David Chao (G).
Damascus: Damascus HS, Jennifer (Polly) Jones (S), William Wade (L), Angela Wyman (G), Kristin Alban (F).
Ellicott City: Mt. Hebron HS, Tracey Day (S), Edith Kealey (G), Laura Snader (F).
Frederick: Hood C, Luz M. DeBrosse (S).
Garrison: Garrison Forest S, Shalini Sharma (F).
Hagerstown: South Hagerstown HS, Leslie McAdoo (F), Christy Eshelman (S). **North Hagerstown HS,** Beth Murrary (F).
Kensington: Albert Einstein HS, Robert Brown (F).
Monkton: Hereford MS, Kira R. Peterson (F).
Salisbury: James M. Bennett SHS, Mark Handy (F), Elizabeth Holder (L), Kenneth Moore (S).
Towson: Notre Dame Prep S, Edith Anne Urbanck (G), Victoria Matter (S), Kathleen Leopold (F).
Upper Marlboro: Queen Anne S, Jeff Shulden (F), Aubrey Baden (S).
Westminster: Westminster SHS, Mark Hamme (G).
Williamsport: Williamsport HS, Erin M. Miller (S), Tammy Socks (G), Laura Shane (F).
MASSACHUSETTS
Attleboro: Attleboro HS, James Carty (F), Catherine Gallivan (G), Elizabeth Leroux (L), Nelia Pacheco (S).
Bridgewater: Bridgewater-Raynham Reg HS, Ellen Brennan (S), Yvonne Pickett (L).
Byfield: Triton Reg, Marisa Pedulla (F).
Deerfield: Eaglebrook School, John Eagleton (F), Michael Magee (S).
Groton: Groton-Dunstable Reg Sec S, Kelly Vachon (F), Melissa Rice (L).
Haverhill: Haverhill HS, Kristine Perry (L), Stephen Raymond (G), Michael Pierce (I), Francis Selvaggio (S), Marie Salter (F).
Hingham: Hingham Pub S, Paul Needham (L), John Sargent (S).
Lawrence: Lawrence HS, Cynthia Quaglietta (S).
Mattapoisett: Old Rochester Reg HS, Christine Knight (S), Audra L. Ouellette (F).
Milton: Milton HS, Ursula Jackson (F), Kimberly O'Neill (S).
Needham: Needham HS, Mathieu Chapuis (I), Danay Giannopoulas (F), Erin Glasheen (S), Maria Mancini (L).
North Dartmouth: Southeastern Mass U, Therese Letourneau (F).
Quincy: Quincy HS, Renee Picard (S). **Eastern Nazarene C,** Elizabeth Schuster (F).
Sudbury: Lincoln-Sudbury Reg HS, Theresa A. Hadlock (S), Elspeth Slayter (R), Joseph Delregno (L), Lynn Garth (F).
Tyngsboro: Tyngsboro JSHS, Kathryn Julie Ross (F).
Walpole: Walpole HS, Bruce Sacerdote (S), Paula Nannicelli (F), Kristin Friedholm (L).
Wellesley: Wellesley HS, Paul Glauthier (F), Andrea Donlon (S), Ariane McCoy (L). **Wellesley C,** Ruth Randolph (S).
West Springfield: West Springfield SHS, Alexandra Reynolds (F), Denise Plourde (G), Tina Dultz (I), Karen Ormsby (L), Christine Kuralt (S).
Winchester: Winchester HS, Penny Kapanika (I), Janet Weylman (G), Jennifer Tobiason (F).
Worcester: Ralph C. Mahar Reg S, Ruth Potee (S).
Wrentham: King Philip Reg HS, Marie Waters (L), Michelle Reid (F), Anita Carson (S).
MICHIGAN
Detroit: Cass Technical HS, Lillian Marzoug (L), Freya Murphy (S), Zakir Sahul (F).
Elk Rapids: Elk Rapids HS, Denise Marie Messing (F).
Farmington: Mercy HS, Katie Donlon (S).
Fraser: Fraser HS, Kari Ehrke (F), Jacquelyn Rudnicki (S).
Gladwin: Gladwin HS, Jenny Peters (S).
Sault Ste. Marie: Sault Ste. Marie Area HS, Jillian Cook (F).
MISSISSIPPI
Biloxi: Biloxi HS, Grace Jones (S).
Pascagoula: Pascagoula HS, Beverly Henshaw (F), Craig Concannon (G), Guilpana Solitario (S).

MISSOURI
Independence: Van Horn HS, Pamela Rudy (G), Carolyn Bailey (F), Larry Hackleman (S).
NEW HAMPSHIRE
Concord: Concord HS, Holly Carlson (S), Angela Morin (F), Karen C. Lassey (G), Derek Duff (L). **Rundlett JHS,** John Blackadar (L), Abigail Wildman (F), Amy S. Turgeon (S), Richard Harrison (G).
Hanover: Hanover HS, Drew Whitney (F), Mark Joseph (G), Sarah Duncan (L).
NEW JERSEY
Annadale: North Hunterdon HS, Philip Covitz (R), Lisa Orlandini (L), Darlene Marie Dubeck (S), Lisa Sweet (G), Kristen L. Conrad (F).
Atco: Edgewood SHS, Wendy Lieberman (F).
Bayonne: Bayonne HS, Adrianne Tovar (S).
Bayville: Central Reg HS, Kathleen Laing (S), Carol Roberts (F).
Beverly Heights: Governor Livingston Reg HS, Robert Edge (S), Sue Lynn Chang (F), Nancy Boll (G).
Bloomfield: Bloomfield HS, Roman Dreyer (S).
Bound Brook: Bound Brook HS, Kathy Thomas (L), Kathy Thomas (F).
Caldwell: Caldwell C, Julia Pena (F).
Carney's Point: Penns Grove HS, Steven Bouvier (G), Allison Whitney (L), Thomas Garrett (S).
Chatham: Chatham Boro HS, Chris Phillips (S), Elvire Volpicelli (F), Michael Kanaley (L), James Saltzman (G).
Cinnamison: Cinnamison HS, William Allen Smith (S), Carl Albert Johnson (F), Richard James Keevey (G).
Clark: Arthur L. Johnson Reg HS, Michael Cargill (I), John Araujo (S), Robin Ridge (G).
Demarest: Northern Valley Regional HS, Michael Ramadas (G), Kay Levine (I), Jennifer Huse (F), Paul Nyfenger (S).
Denville: Morris Knolls HS, Patricia Lutz (G), Michele Kortvelyesy (F), Kimberly Harris (S).
East Brunswick: East Brunswick HS, Connie Hassett (G), Todd Feldman (L), Todd Girshon (S), Sandra Smith (F).
Edison: John P. Stevens HS, Judy Bornstein (S), Beth Heller (F). **Edison Township HS,** Michelle Hynes (F), Pratik Patel (S).
Elmwood Park: Elmwood Park Mem HS, Franco Scolaro (I), Catherine Biviano (S), Tatiana Tomei (F).
Engelwood: Dwight-Englewood S, Scott Anagnoste (F), Holly Borenstein (S), Heather Wood (L).
Freehold: Freehold Township HS, Rebecca Felsen (F), Dawn Richmond (L), Suzanne Bibona (S).
Hackensack: Hackensack HS, Amy Turizo (F), Karen Bressan (S), Christina Bresaz (I).
Hightstown: The Peddie S, Michelle A. Annarella (F), Timothy J. Acito (S), Myra Zaharchuk (L).
Holmdel: Holmdel HS, Sarah Moessinger (S), Catherine Ford (F), Alissa Nurnberger (G). **St. John Vianney HS,** Rachel Canton (F), Mary Ann Hansen (S), Dina Marie Perrino (L), Kari Depol (G).
Iselin: John F. Kennedy Mem HS, Cheryl Butchko (F), Paul Urban (S), Donna Teator (G).
Kenilworth: David Brearly HS, Rosalba Latorre (I), J. Christopher Cardoso (S).
Linden: Soehl MS, Victoria Cassiba (S), Stacy Arlotta (G), Denise Dobos (F). **Linden HS,** Nancy Pohl (G). **McManus MS,** Janet Kornberger (F), Mayte Martinez (G), Michele Chomiszak (S).
Lodi: Lodi HS, Marie Marco (F), Maria Petrillo (I), Scott Impomeni (S).
Lyndhurst: Lyndhurst HS, Diane Ulrich (S), Catherine Kranich (F), Dino Mezzina (I), Dana Marion Rotella (G).
Lakehurst: Manchester Twp HS, Laura Delabar (F), Wendy Darby (S).
Maplewood: Columbia HS, Christine Fiumara (L), Luba Tymczyna (G), Katherine Profeta (F), Margaret Balazs (S), Patricia Derme (I).
Metuchen: Metuchen HS, Rebecca Stern (F), Renee Hall (G), David Kirtman (S).
Millburn: Millburn SHS, Piera Bianco (I), Matthew Morchower (F), Loren Walensky (S).
Montclair: Montclair HS, Britta Padberg (G), Oliver Galm (L), Jane Schuchinski (S), Andrew Weislogel (F).
Morristown: Villa Walsh Acad, Grace Ann Franzese (I),

Jennifer McGovern (S). **Frelinghuyen Junior S,** Edward Yamoza (S), Tara Parmiter (F).
New Brunswick: New Brunswick HS, Arelis Taveras (ESL), Sonia Serrano (F), Arelis Taveras (S), Jane Lee (L).
New Milford: New Milford HS, Ronald Levinson (S), Stephen Karolokian (F).
Newton: Kittatinny Reg HS, Christina Vela (S).
North Arlington: Queen of Peace HS, Annemarie Cross (S), Gina Marie O'Neill (I), Christine Goldrick (F).
North Brunswick: North Brunswick Twp HS, Melissa Previte (G), Melissa Previte (I).
Oradell: Bergan Catholic HS, Joseph Brendan Kroculick (S), James Christopher Mendler (I), Christopher Anthony Meyers (F).
Palisades Park: Palisades Park J-SHS, Vikki Mesropian (F), Celestina Maucieri (I).
Paramus: Paramus HS, Brian Becker (S), Arthur Chaney (L), Elana Klein (H), David Luongo (I), Thomas Conroy (F), Doris Duwe (G).
Parsippany: Parsippany Hills HS, Leonard Guzman (S), Vivian Shen (G), Cynthia Harvey (F), Robin Hosig (I).
Plainfield: Plainfield HS, Luis Freire (F), Deborah Warner (S).
Pompton Plains: Pequannock Twp HS, Michelle Hopper (L), Karen Hitchcock (S).
Princeton: St. Joseph's Prep Seminary, Laszlo Stojalowsky (S).
Princeton Junction: West Junction-Plainsboro HS, Stephanie Churn (G), Maureen O'Driscoll (S), Jennifer Nolan (F).
Riverside: Riverside HS, Mary Zoldi (S), David Arey (F).
Rockaway: Morris Hills HS, Robin L. Barton (F), Bonnie G. Weissenburger (G), Deborah A. Reuther (S).
Rumson: Rumson-Fair Haven Reg HS, Cynthia Bansak (F), Jennifer Ingle (S).
Somerset: Franklin HS, Donald Sweeney (S), Kelly Ann McGann (R), Judy Hauss (L), Helen Eisma (G), Beth Babey (F), Sandra Hayes (I). **Rutgers Prep,** Julia Lenaghan (S), Joshua Shi Blume (F).
South Orange: Marylawn of the Oranges, Nancy Feula (L), Olive Lee (S), Janet Scuorzo (F).
Succasuna: Roxbury HS, Michelle DiEllo (S), Michael Stroble (G).
Summit: Summit HS, Kelly Ryan (L). **Oratory Prep,** Aidan Wasley (F), Robert Zebick (L), James Kearney (S).
Tinton Falls: Monmouth Reg HS, Jeannie Wu (F), Michael Nason (G), Lajuana Kelly (L), Hillary Harwood (S).
Toms River: Toms River HS North, Christopher Cerone (S). **Toms River HS South,** Sherry Lehr (F), Patrick Winkler (G).
Trenton: McCorristin Catholic HS, Luz Maria Vazquez (S), Portia Freeman (F), Dino Sorrento (I). **Ewing HS,** Cheryl Donnelly (S), Margaret Sancho (F).
Vineland: Vineland HS South, Donald Weinstein (F), Tracy Walters (G), Marie Jost (I), Tammy Reger (L), Lisa Batt (S).
West Orange: West Orange HS, Amy King (F), Jacqueline Peck (S), Jeffrey DeCagna (I).
NEW YORK
Amherst: Amherst Central HS, Michael Atleson (F), John Haefner (L), Laura Mazziotti (S), Valerie Case (G).
Brooklyn: Poly Prep CDS, Christopher McGibbon (F).
Castleton: Maple Hill HS, Michael Jenkins (F).
Delhi: Delaware Acad and Central S, David Michael Odell (G).
Elmont: Elmont Memorial HS, Vollard Bastien (F), Christopher Crawford (S).
Farmingdale: Farmingdale SHS, Gina Cammarano (F), Tanja Preussher (G), Ronald Dodson (I), Maria Mingione (S).
Franklin Square: Valley Stream North HS, Laura Lacchia (F), Elizabeth Perrin (S).
Hartsdale: Woodlands HS, Victoria Holloway (F), Norma Sandoval (S), Ana Dominguez (I).
Henrietta: James E. Sperry HS, Deanna Miller (L), Kirsten Bugenhagen (G), Robin Kassmann (S), Karen Segar (F). **Charles H. Roth HS,** Albert Fulton (G), Yvonne Murphy (S), Susan Stanton (F).

Jamaica: Hillcrest HS, Dawn Martin (S).
Kings Park: William T. Rogers JHS, Steven Lustig (S), Mary Pearl Cavero (F).
Mexico: Mexico Acad and Central S, Donna Duggan (S). **Mexico HS,** Terry McAuslan (G). **Mexico MS,** Jill Smith (G).
Mineola: Mineola HS, Kerri McDevitt (S), Gina Mastrantoni (L), Yi-Shin Lai (F).
New Rochelle: The Ursuline S, Yvette Manessis (S).
Old Westbury: The Wheatley S, Jacqueline Starr (L), Caroline Lupatelli (I), Laura D'Amato (S), Jennifer Freiman (F).
Orangeburg: Tappan Zee HS, Richard Villanueva (G), Alina Roman (F).
Orchard Park: Orchard Park MS, Rachel Murphy (S), Kathryn Ackerman (F).
Pelham: Pelham Mem HS, Diana Scharrer (F), Alexander Schwab (S), Jennifer Jackino (I).
Rochester: Brighton HS, Karla Yessenow (S), Robert Nelson (R), Daniel Panner (F), Matt Kittelberger (G), Heather Griggs (L).
Rockville Centre: South Side HS, Leonard Landesberg (F), Christine Horowitz (S).
Roslyn: Roslyn HS, Emily Peters (F), Stefanie Rosenberg (I), Todd Eagle (S).
Schenectady: Niskayuna HS, Michael Eddo (F), Anna Berkenblit (L), Mark Ontkush (G), Kimberley Stevens (S).
Seneca Falls: Mynderse Acad, H. John Manzari (S), William Leonard (F).
Shoreham: Shoreham-Wading River HS, Deborah Jensen (F).
Staten Island: St. John Villa Acad, Diana Lo Guzzo (I), Christina Scattaglia (S).
Valley Stream: Valley Stream Central HS, Michael Spera (S), William Kirschner (G), Robert Kinney (F), Sonia Blangiardo (I).
Wantagh: Wantagh HS, Mark Mellynchuck (S), Daniel Powers (F).
West Henrietta: Rush-Henrietta JHS, Kris Minor (F), Bick Truong (S).
Watervliet: Watervliet HS, Jason Santora (F), Carol DiBacco (R), Linda Dean (S), Colleen Harbour (G).
NORTH CAROLINA
High Point: High Point C, Alicia Wright (F), Kelly Brisentine (S).
OHIO
Bellaire: Bellaire HS, Josy Noice (F), Dawna Fisher (S).
Cincinnati: Colerain SHS, Melissa Fehl (G), Beatrice Belcher (F).
Cincinnati: U of Cincinnati, Kimberly Taylor (Swedish).
Cleveland Heights: Beaumont S for Girls, Catherine Keefe (L), Kimberly Cleveland (S), Jeanine Maddox (F).
Martins Ferry: Martins Ferry HS, Rachelle Talasis (F).
Mt. Vernon: Mt. Vernon Nazarene C, Aaron Thompson (S).
Toledo: Central Catholic HS, Rebecca Beins (G), Kathleen Berry (S).
Toledo: Whitmer HS, Christine Lillibridge (S), Debbie Schwieder (G), Amy Alexander (F).
Wapakoneta: Blume JHS, Jodi Brincefield (S), Ryung Chun (L), Jennifer Prater (F).
PENNSYLVANIA
Abington: Abington HS, Neil Gever (F), Curtis Equi (S), Robert Maxwell (L), Sharon Ritter (G), Loredana Caso (I).
Aliquippa: Hopewell SHS, Alana Karle (L), Tedine Ranich (F), Kathy Malloy (G), Timothy Toomey (S).
Allentown: Allentown Central HS, Elizabeth Lavelle (G), Frank Smiegel (L), Kim Schwartz (S), Carolyn Huber (F).
Alverton: Southmoreland SHS, Gordon Bradley Stewart (S).
Camp Hill: Cedar Cliff HS, Vivienne Shen (L), Hylda Hendriksma (F), Karin Johnson (G), Stephen Rehrer (S).
Fairless Hills: Pennsbury HS, Anne Kenney (F), Joseph Kiefer (G), Daniel Poremba (S).
Flourtown: Mt. St. Joseph Acad, Elizabeth Burke (L).
Freeland: MMI Prep S, Jill Morgan (S).
Jenkintown: Jenkintown HS, Evelyn Furse (S), Leslie Albright (F).

Latrobe: Greater Latrobe SHS, Kim Mills (G), Amy Leonard (S), Kelly Smolleck (F).

Malvern: Villa Maria Acad, Laura Walsh (F).

Meadville: Allegheny C, Wendy Parker (S), Brenna Bond (F), Joel Nagel (G).

Merion: Merion Mercy Acad, Margaret Harley (S).

Morrisdale: West Branch Area HS, Paula Shedlock (S).

Newtown Square: Marple Newtown SHS, Mary Claire Vogrin (F), Diane Benfer (S), Lisa Streit (G).

Philadelphia: Abraham Lincoln HS, Robert Belz (F). **George Washington HS,** Sherri Weiss (H), Eric E. Horvath (G), Brett Singer (S), Todd Dechter (F). **St. Joseph's U,** Lisa Marie Santore (I), Mary Kateri Carver (F), Mary Morris (G), Mary Beth Ziff (S).

Reading: Albright C, Karen E. Rismiller (G), Janis Wood (F), Christina Hedin (S).

State College: State College Area SHS, Penelope Smith (G), Kelly Swanson (F), Joni Black (R), Edie Tsong (S).

Stoneboro: Lakeview HS, Teresa Yeager (L), Janetta Marie Sauer (S), Rebecca Shawgo (F).

Tyrone: Tyrone Area HS, Terri Lynn Longenecker (F), Brian Clark (L), Becky Dunkel (S).

Warminster: Archbishop Wood Girls' HS, Kimberly Benninghoff (S), Diane Monaghan (F), Christine Lang (G).

West Chester: East HS, Megan Bonsall (F). **Henderson HS,** Donna Fort (G), Cynthia Cluff (S), Deborah Greger (L), Gina DeMarco (F).

West Lawn: Wilson HS, Pamela Schwartz (F), Wendi Witman (G), Kimberly Beattie (S).

Wyncote: Cheltenham HS, Julie Phillips (F), Charlee Leimberg (S), Nancy Rothbard (L).

RHODE ISLAND

Cranston: Cranston HS East, Gerald Forcier (L), Frank Costa (G), Debbie Lee (S), Jennifer Champa (F).

Narragansett: Narragansett HS, Michelle Foley (F), Kelly Ann Degnan (I), Adrian Owens (S).

Newport: Salve Regina HS, Maria Elena Lara (S).

Pawtucket: Saint Raphael Acad, Dianne Desjardins (F), Demetrios Tsakanos (S). **Tolman SHS,** Lisa LaScola (F), Carla Lopes (Portuguese), Michelle Molhan (S).

Providence: La Salle Acad, James Erinakes (S), Peter DiLullo (I), Anthony Matarese (F). **Classical HS,** Bryony Romer (F), Maria Nardi (I), Raymond J. Deacon (L), Christine Incera (S).

Riverside: St. Mary Acad Bay View, Helene Rita Arcand (F).

Smithfield: Smithfield HS, Georgia Keene (F).

Wakefield: South Kingston HS, Carl Crifalconi (L), Mary Peterson (S), Carolyn Tacey (I), Jason Craven (F).

Warwick: Pilgrim HS, Karen DeGenova (I), Peter Miller (R), Daniel Sheehan (S). **Toll Gate HS,** Melissa Mansolillo (S), Alan Brown (F), Kerstin LeMaire (G), Tod Garfinkel (I).

SOUTH CAROLINA

Spartanburg: Spartanburg HS, Rebecca Anne Ross (S). **Dorman HS,** Deidra Shelton (S).

SOUTH DAKOTA

Sioux Falls: North American Baptist Seminary, Jerry Keith Mathis (Hebrew), Gordon Stork (Greek).

TENNESSEE

Memphis: St. Agnes Acad, Mindy Keyes (F). **Fairley HS,** Isiah McCray (S).

TEXAS

Dallas: The Greenhill S, Elena Koutras (F).

UTAH

Kanab: Kanab HS, Nicole Bonham (S).

VERMONT

Brattleboro: Brattleboro Union HS, Jennifer Estrella (G), Kim Abell (S), Kristin Anderson (F).

Essex Junction: Essex Junction Ed Center, Susan Pietryka (F), Serge J. Olszanskyj (S), Peter Quintin (L).

VIRGINIA

Arlington: Bishop Denis J. O'Connell HS, James O'Donnell (L), Ramon Madan (S), Steve Kulm (G), Colleen McGowan (F).

Bedford: Liberty HS, David Marshall Clark (F).

Mineral: Louisa County HS, Mary Alice Buhrer (S).

Radford: Belle Heth Elem S, Lauren Elizabeth Cogswell (F).

Richmond: Douglas S. Freeman HS, Anne Macon Smith (F), Kelly Shifflett (L), Jeanie Kim (S). **Mills E. Godwin HS,** Thomas Stahl (L), Susan Oehler (G), Lee Campbell (F). **Manchester HS,** Jean Renee Burch (F).

South Boston: Halifax County SHS, Lisa M. Tucker (S), Emily Anne Moore (L), William L. Gore (F).

WISCONSIN

Appleton: Xavier HS, Cuong Nguyen (F), Heidi Eckert (G), Stephen Wisnefski (S).

Waukesha: Waukesha North HS, Rachel Gross (S). **Central HS,** Wendy Nemyer (G).

WEST VIRGINIA

Dunbar: Dunbar HS, Lisa Snodgrass (F).

Fairmont: Fairmont SHS, Jennifer Brumage (F), John Bailey (L), Todd Commodore (S).

WYOMING

Casper: Natrona County HS, Marisa Hauck (L), John Goss (G), Andelyn Olsen (F), Michelle Fuguere (S).

Sheridan: Sheridan HS, Kathleen Laya (F), Leanne Schultz (S).

Northeast Conference Officers and Directors Since 1954

Andersson, Theodore [Yale U.]* U. of Texas, Director 1954-56.

Andrews, Oliver, Jr., U. of Connecticut, Director 1971-74.

Arndt, Richard, Columbia U., Director 1961.

Arsenault, Philip E., Montgomery County (MD.) Public Schools, Local Chairman 1967, 1970; Director 1971, 1973-74; Vice Chairman 1975; Conference Chairman 1976.

Atkins, Jeannette, Staples (Westport, CT) HS, Director 1962-65.

Baird, Janet, U. of Maryland, Local Chairman 1974.

Baker, Robert M., Middlebury C., Director 1987-90.

Bashour, Dora, [Hunter C.], Secretary 1963-1964; Recording Secretary 1965-68.

Baslaw, Annette S., [Teachers C.], Hunter C., Local Chairman 1973.

Bayerschmidt, Carl F., Columbia U., Conference Chairman 1961.

Bennett, Ruth, Queens C., Local Chairman 1975-76.

Bertin, Gerald A., Rutgers U., Local Chairman 1960.

Berwald, Jean-Pierre, U. of Massachusetts, Director 1980-83.

Bird, Thomas E., Queens C., Editor 1967-68; Director 1969.

Bishop, G. Reginald, Jr., Rutgers U., Editor 1960, 1965; Director 1961-62, 1965, 1968; Vice Chairman 1966; Conference Chairman 1967.

Bishop, Thomas, W., New York U., Local Chairman 1965.

Born, Warren C., [ACTFL], Editor 1974-79.

Bostroem, Kyra, Westover School, Director 1961.

Bottiglia, William F., MIT, Editor 1957, 1962-63; Director 1964.

Bourque, Jane M., [Stratford (CT) Public Schools] Mt. Vernon (NY) Public Schools, Director 1974-75; Vice Chairman 1976; Conference Chairman 1977.

Brée, Germaine, [New York U., U. of Wisconsin] Wake Forest U., Conference Chairman 1955. Editor 1955.

Brod, Richard I., MLA, Consultant to the Chairman, 1983, Director 1985-88.

Brooks, Nelson†, [Yale U.], Director 1954-57, 1960-61; Vice Chairman 1959.

Brown, Christine L., [West Hartford (CT) Public Schools] Glastonbury (CT) Public Schools, Director 1982-85, Vice Chairman 1986, Conference Chairman 1987.

Byrnes, Heidi, Georgetown U., Director 1985-88.

Cadoux, Remunda† [Hunter C.], Vice Chairman 1969; Conference Chairman 1970.

Campbell, Hugh, [Roxbury Latin School] Rocky Hill Country Day School, Director 1966-67.

Churchill, J. Frederick, Hofstra U., Director 1966-67; Local Chairman 1971-72.

Ciotti, Marianne C., [Vermont State Department of Education, Boston U.] Barre (VT) Public Schools, Director 1967.

Cincinnato, Paul D., Farmingdale (NY) Public Schools, Director 1974-77; Vice Chairman 1978, Conference Chairman 1979.

Cintas, Pierre F., [Dalhousie U.], Penn. St. U.-Ogontz, Director 1976-79.

Cipriani, Anita A., Hunter C. Elem. Sch., Director 1986-89.

Clark, John L.D., [CAL] DLI, Director 1976-1978, Vice Chairman 1979, Conference Chairman 1980.

Clark, Richard P., Newton (MA) HS, Director 1967.

Clemens, Brenda Frazier, [Rutgers U., U. of Connecticut] Howard U., Director 1972-1975.

Cobb, Martha, Howard U., Director 1976-77; Recording Secretary 1978.

Covey, Delvin L., [Montclair State C.] Spring Arbor C., Director 1964-65.

Crawford, Dorothy B., Philadelphia HS for Girls, Conference Chairman 1956.

Dahme, Lena F., Hunter C., Local Chairman 1958; Director 1959.

Darcey, John M., West Hartford (CT) Public Schools, Director 1978-81. Vice Chairman 1982, Conference Chairman 1983, Editor 1987.

Del Olmo, Filomena Peloro, [Hackensack (NJ) Public Schools] Fairleigh Dickinson U., Director 1960-63.

De Napoli, Anthony J., Wantagh (NY) Public Schools, Local Co-chairman 1980-82, 87, Director 1982-85.

Di Donato, Robert, MIT, Consultant to the Chairman 1986.

Didsbury, Robert, Weston (CT) JHS, Director 1966-69.

Dodge, James, W., Middlebury C., Editor 1971-73; Secretary-Treasurer 1974-88.

Dostert, Leon E.†, [Georgetown U.] Occidental C., Conference Chairman 1959.

Dufau, Micheline, U. of Massachusetts, Director 1976-79.

Dye, Joan C., Hunter C., Local Co-chairman 1978.

Eaton, Annette, Howard U., Director 1967-70.

Eddy, Frederick D.†, [U. of Colorado], Editor 1959; Director 1960.

Eddy, Peter A., [CAL/ERIC], CIA, Director 1977-78.

Edgerton, Mills F., Jr., Bucknell U., Editor 1969; Director 1970; Vice Chairman 1971; Conference Chairman 1972.

Elling, Barbara E., SUNY at Stony Brook, Director 1980-83.

Feindler, Joan L., Easton Williston (NY) Public Schools, Director 1969-71; Vice Chairman 1972; Conference Chairman 1973.

Flaxman, Seymour, [New York U.] City C. of New York, Editor 1961; Director 1962.

Freeman, Stephen A., [Middlebury C.], Director 1957-60.

Fulton, Renee J., New York City Board of Education, Director 1955.

Gaarder, A. Bruce, USOE, Director 1971-74.

Galloway, Vicki B., ACTFL, Consultant to the Chairman 1985.

Geary, Edward J., [Harvard U.] Bowdoin C., Conference Chairman 1962.

Geno, Thomas H., U. of Vermont, Director 1975-76; Vice Chairman 1977; Conference Chairman 1978, Recording Secretary 1979, Editor 1980-81.

Gilman, Margaret†, Bryn Mawr C., Editor 1956.

Glaude, Paul M., N.Y. State Department of Education, Director 1963-66.

Golden, Herbert H., Boston U., Director 1962.

Grew, James H., [Phillips Acad.], Director 1966-69.

Hartie, Robert W., Queens C., Local Chairman 1966.

Harrison, John S., Baltimore County (MD) Public Schools, Local Co-Chairman 1979, 1983; Director 1983-86.

Hayden, Hilary, O.S.B., St. Anselm's Abbey School, Vice Chairman 1970; Conference Chairman 1971.

Hayes, Alfred S.†, CAL, Vice Chairman 1963; Conference Chairman 1964.

Hernandez, Juana A., Hood C., Director 1978-81.

Holzmann, Albert W., Rutgers U., Director 1960.

Jalbert, Emile H. [Thayer Acad.] Berkshire Comm. C., Local Chairman 1962.

Jarvis, Gilbert A., Ohio State U., Editor 1984.

Jebe, Suzanne, [Guilford (CT) HS], Minn. Dept. of Ed., Director 1975-76; Recording Secretary 1977.

Johnston, Marjorie C. [USOE], Local Chairman 1964.

Jones, George W., Jr., Norfolk (VA) Public Schools, Director 1977-80.

Kahn, Timothy M., S. Burlington (VT) HS, Director 1979-82.

Keesee, Elizabeth, USOE, Director 1966-70.

Kellenberger, Hunter†, [Brown U.], Conference Chairman 1954; Editor 1954.

Kennedy, Dora F., Prince George's County (MD) Public Schools, Director 1985-88.

Kesler, Robert, Phillips Exeter Acad., Director 1957.

Kibbe, Doris E., Montclair State C., Director 1968-69.

Kramsch, Claire J., MIT, Director 1984-87.

La Follette, James E., Georgetown, U., Local chairman

1959.

La Fontaine, Hernan, New York City Board of Education, Director 1972.

Lenz, Harold, Queens C., Local Chairman 1961.

Lepke, Helen S., [Kent State U.] Clarion U. of Pennsylvania, Director 1981-1984; Vice Chairman 1985; Conference Chairman 1986.

Lester, Kenneth A., Connecticut State Dept. of Education, Recording Secretary 1982.

Levy, Harry†, [Hunter C.] Fordham U., Editor 1958; Director 1959-61; Conference Chairman 1963.

Levy, Stephen L., [New York City Board of Education] Roslyn (NY) Public Schools, Local Co-Chairman 1978, 80-82, 87, Director 1980-83; Vice Chairman 1984; Conference Chairman 1985.

Lieberman, Samuel, Queens C., Director 1966-69.

Liskin-Gasparro, Judith E., [ETS] Middlebury C., Recording Secretary 1984; Director 1986-89.

Lipton, Gladys C., [New York City Board of Education], Anne Arundel County (MD) Public Schools, Director 1973-76.

Lloyd, Paul M., U. of Pennsylvania, Local Chairman 1963.

Locke, William N.†, MIT, Conference Chairman 1957; Director 1958-59.

MacAllister, Archibald T.†, [Princeton U.] Director 1955-57; 1959-61.

Masciantonio, Rudolph, School District of Philadelphia, Director 1969-71.

Mead, Robert G., Jr., U. of Connecticut, Director 1955; Editor 1966; Vice Chairman 1967; Conference Chairman 1968, Editor 1982-83.

Mesnard, André, Barnard C., Director 1954-55.

Micozzi, Arthur L., Baltimore County (MD) Public Schools, Local Committee Chairman, 1977, 79, 83, 86; Director 1979-82.

Mirsky, Jerome G., [Jericho (NY) SHS], Shoreham-Wading River (NY) HS, Director 1970-73; Vice Chairman 1974; Conference Chairman 1975.

Nelson, Robert J., [U. of Pennsylvania] U. of Illinois, Director 1965-68.

Neuse, Werner, [Middlebury C.], Director 1954-56.

Nionakis, John P., Hingham (MA) Public Schools, Director 1984-87.

Obstfeld, Roland, Northport (NY) HS, Recording Secretary 1976.

Omaggio, Alice C., U. of Illinois, Editor 1985.

Owens, Doris Barry, West Hartford (CT) Public Schools, Recording Secretary 1983.

Pane, Remigio U., Rutgers U., Conference Chairman 1960.

Paquette, André, [Middlebury C.] Laconia (NH) Public Schools, Director 1963-66; Vice Chairman 1968; Conference Chairman 1969.

Parks, Carolyn, [U. of Maryland] French Int'l. S., Recording Secretary 1981.

Perkins, Jean, Swarthmore C., Treasurer 1963-64; Conference Chairman 1966.

Petrosino, Vince J., Baltimore (MD) City Sch., Local Chairman 1986.

Phillips, June K., Indiana U. of Pennsylvania, Director 1979-82, Vice Chairman 1983; Conference Chairman 1984, Consultant to the Chairman 1986.

Prochoroff, Marina, [MLA Materials Center], Director 1962-64.

Ramirez, Mario L., School District of Philadelphia, Director 1974.

Reilly, John H., Queens C., Local Chairman 1968-69; Director 1970.

Renjilian-Burgy, Joy, Wellesley C., Director 1987-90.

Riley, Kerry, U. of Maryland, Consultant to the Chairman 1986.

Rochefort, Frances A., Cranston (RI) Public Schools, Director 1986-89.

Russo, Gloria M., [U. of Virginia], Director 1983-86.

Sandstrom, Eleanor L., School District of Philadelphia, Director 1975-78.

Selvi, Arthur M., Central Connecticut State C., Director 1954.

Senn, Alfred, U. of Pennsylvania, Director 1956.

Serafino, Robert, New Haven (CT) Public Schools, Director 1969-73.

Sheppard, Douglas C., [SUNY at Buffalo] Arizona State U., Director 1968-71.

Shilaeff, Ariadne, Wheaton C., Director 1978-80.

Shuster, George N.†, [U. of Notre Dame], Conference Chairman 1958.

Simches, Seymour O., Tufts U., Director 1962-65; Vice Chairman 1965.

Sims, Edna N., U. of D.C., Director 1981-84.

Sister Margaret Pauline, Emmanuel C., Director 1957, 1965-68; Recording Secretary 1969-1975.

Sister Margaret Therese, Trinity C., Director 1959-60.

Sister Mary Pierre, Georgian Court C., Director 1961-64.

Sousa, Helen Candi, West Hartford (CT) Public Schools, Director 1987-90.

Sparks, Kimberly, Middlebury C., Director 1969-72.

Starr, Wilmarth H., [U. of Maine] New York U., Director 1960-63, 1966; Vice Chairman 1964; Conference Chairman 1965.

Steer, Alfred G., Jr., Columbia U., Director 1961.

Stein, Jack M.†, [Harvard U.], Director 1962.

Stracener, Rebecca J., Edison (NJ) Public Schools, Director 1984-87.

Tamarkin, Toby, Manchester (CT) Comm. C., Director 1977-80, Vice Chairman 1981, Conference Chairman 1982, Recording Secretary 1987.

Thompson, Mary P., [Glastonbury (CT) Public Schools], Director 1957-62.

Trivelli, Remo J., U. of Rhode Island, Director 1981-84.

Tursi, Joseph, [SUNY at Stony Brook], Editor 1970; Director 1971-72; Vice Chairman 1973; Conference Chairman 1974.

Valette, Rebecca, Boston C., Director 1972-75.

Vasquez-Amaral, Jose, Rutgers U., Director 1960.

Walker, Richard H., Bronxville (NY) HS, Director 1954.

Walsh, Donald D.†, [MLA], Director 1954; Secretary-Treasurer 1965-73.

Warner, Pearl M., New York City Public Schools, Recording Secretary 1985.

White, Emile Margaret, [District of Columbia Public Schools], Director 1955-58.

Williamson, Richard C., Bates C., Director 1983-86. Vice Chairman 1987, Conference Chairman 1988.

Wing, Barbara H., U. of New Hampshire, Editor 1986.

Woodford, Protase E., Educational Testing Service, Director 1982-85.

Yakobson, Helen B., George Washington U., Director 1959-60.

Zimmer-Loew, Helene, [N.Y. State Education Dept.] AATG, Director 1977-79; Vice Chairman 1980; Conference Chairman 1981.

---

* Where a change of academic affiliation is known, the earlier address appears in brackets.
† Deceased